D0218537

FROM
READING
TO
WRITING

KAREN BLANCHARD

LYNN BONESTEEL

Series Editor
LINDA ROBINSON FELLAG

PEARSON
Longman

From Reading to Writing 2

Copyright © 2010 by Pearson Education, Inc.
All rights reserved.
No part of this publication may be reproduced, stored in a retrieval system, or transmitted in any form or by any means, electronic, mechanical, photocopying, recording, or otherwise, without the prior permission of the publisher.

Pearson Education, 10 Bank Street, White Plains, NY 10606

Staff credits: The people who made up the *From Reading to Writing 2* team, representing editorial, production, design, and manufacturing, are Eleanor Barnes, Rosa Chapinal, Dave Dickey, Françoise Leffler, Martha McGaughey, Massimo Rubini, Kim Steiner, Jennifer Stem, Jane Townsend, Paula Van Ells, Patricia Wosczyk, and Adina Zoltan.

Text composition: ElectraGraphics, Inc.
Text font: 11 pt New Aster
Photo credits: See page 195.

Library of Congress Cataloging-in-Publication Data
Bonesteel, Lynn.
   From reading to writing / Lynn Bonesteel . . . [et al.].
      p. cm.
   Includes index.
   ISBN 0-13-205066-8—ISBN 0-13-612780-0—ISBN 0-13-233096-2—
ISBN 0-13-158867-2 1. English language—Textbooks for foreign speakers. 2. Reading comprehension—Problems, exercises, etc. I. Title.
   PE1128.B6223 2010
   428.2'4—dc22
                                                          2009032265

ISBN-13: 978-0-13-612780-2 (with ProofWriter™)
ISBN-10: 0-13-612780-0 (with ProofWriter™)

ISBN-13: 978-0-13-247403-0 (without ProofWriter™)
ISBN-10: 0-13-247403-4 (without ProofWriter™)

PEARSON LONGMAN ON THE **WEB**

Pearsonlongman.com offers online resources for teachers and students. Access our Companion Websites, our online catalog, and our local offices around the world.

Visit us at **pearsonlongman.com**.

ISBN: 0-13-612780-0 (with ProofWriter™)   2 3 4 5 6 7 8 9 10—V016—13 12 11 10

ISBN: 0-13-247403-4 (without ProofWriter™)   2 3 4 5 6 7 8 9 10—V016—13 12 11 10

Printed in the United States of America

Contents

Introduction   v

Scope and Sequence   x

UNIT ONE   All in the Family   1

Chapter   1   Good Things Come in Fours   2

Chapter   2   Stay-at-Home Dads   12

UNIT TWO   Time to Eat   23

Chapter   3   Pizza around the World   24

Chapter   4   Rachael Ray: Celebrity Chef   35

UNIT THREE   Overcoming Difficulties   45

Chapter   5   Ray Charles   46

Chapter   6   Whoopi Goldberg   57

UNIT FOUR   Places Near and Far   67

Chapter   7   An Anniversary to Remember   68

Chapter   8   Seattle: A Great Place to Live   80

UNIT FIVE   **Keeping Up with Technology**   **91**

     Chapter 9   **Sorry, You've Got Mail**   92

     Chapter 10   **Using YouTube**   103

UNIT SIX   **In Business and at Work**   **113**

     Chapter 11   **The Success of Starbucks**   114

     Chapter 12   **Happiness at Work**   126

UNIT SEVEN   **Music**   **137**

     Chapter 13   **A Gift of Music**   138

     Chapter 14   **Music and Language**   150

UNIT EIGHT   **Education**   **161**

     Chapter 15   **From a Distance**   162

     Chapter 16   **A Healthy Education**   173

Grammar Reference   185

Punctuation and Capitalization   190

Editing Symbols   192

Target Vocabulary   193

Photo Credits   195

Index   196

Introduction

OVERVIEW OF THE SERIES

From Reading to Writing 2 is the first in a four-book series that integrates reading and writing skills and strategies for English language learners. The four-book series includes:

Book 1—Beginning Level

Book 2—High Beginning Level

Book 3—Intermediate Level

Book 4—High Intermediate Level

Reciprocal Reading/Writing Integration

From Reading to Writing provides a complete sequence of high-interest, thematically connected activities that reciprocally integrate reading and writing.

- Students build competence in vocabulary and reading as they move toward writing skill development and completion of a writing assignment.
- Students study the features and language of reading texts, and learn to apply them in their own writing.
- In the same way, writing is integrated into the reading process in accordance with research that suggests writing can enhance reading comprehension (Mlynarcyzk, Spack).

STRUCTURE OF THE BOOKS

Books 1–3 contain eight thematically focused units. Each unit consists of two topically related chapters, divided into two main sections—Reading and Writing—which are linked by a bridge section. Book 4 is organized into nine units. Each unit consists of two thematically connected readings that have accompanying skills and practice activities and are linked by a bridge section, From Reading to Writing. Each reading is also followed by a writing section.

Books 1–3

Each chapter in Books 1–3 includes:

Pre-Reading

Discussion

Vocabulary

Reading

Identifying Main Ideas and Details, Making Inferences

Reading Skill and Practice

Bridge Section—From Reading to Writing

Discussion, Vocabulary review, Journal writing

Writing

Writing Model or Examples

Writing Skills and Practice

Writing Assignment

Writing Process Steps

Book 4

Each unit of Book 4 includes:

Pre-Reading 1

Discussion

Vocabulary

Reading 1

Identifying Main Ideas and Details, Making Inferences

Reading and Vocabulary Skill and Practice

Bridge Section—From Reading to Writing

Discussion and Journal writing

Pre-Reading 2

Discussion

Vocabulary

Reading 2

Identifying Main Ideas and Details, Making Inferences

Writing

Writing Model

Writing Skills and Practice

Writing Assignment

Writing Process Steps

Detailed Explanation of Parts, Books 1–3

Part 1, Reading

In the Pre-Reading section, students build schema by discussing the theme and studying key vocabulary before reading. High-interest readings and lively activities engage students as they develop vocabulary and reading skills and strategies that can be used in their own writing.

Bridge Section—From Reading to Writing

The Reflecting on the Reading activity focuses on content from the reading and how it can be applied to student writing. In some levels, a journal activity provides an opportunity for freewriting. Students can use target vocabulary and explore a question from the reflection activity in depth. Some levels also include exercises to activate vocabulary. Students are asked questions using target vocabulary and are encouraged to use their answers in the upcoming writing assignment.

Part 2, Writing

Writing models and examples as well as writing skills practice allow students to hone their writing skills before they produce their own writing. In the writing assignment, students are led step-by-step through the writing process. This encourages them to gather ideas, focus and organize, and revise and edit their writing. This step-by-step process facilitates collaboration with classmates and the instructor and also promotes self-evaluation of writing.

Benefits to Students

This sequence of activities, common to Books 1–3, has at its core a set of essential competencies for pre-academic English learners that are emphasized throughout the four-book series. Upon completion of the activities, students will be prepared to:

- Recognize and produce a variety of sentences to express ideas (Books 1–2)

- Recognize and utilize the steps in the writing process to produce a composition (Books 2–4)

- Use ideas and language gained from reading in writing and speaking (Books 1–4)

- Organize and write a composition with a main idea and supporting ideas (Books 1–4)

- Recognize and use connectors and other devices that show relationships among ideas in texts (Books 1–4)

- Recognize and express the main idea and supporting details of a reading (Books 1–4)

Vocabulary Focus

The *From Reading to Writing* series also features a strong focus on vocabulary development. The high-frequency vocabulary targeted in each book is derived from three highly recognized vocabulary lists:

- West's *General Service List* (1953) of the 2,000 most frequently used words in English
- Coxhead's *Academic Word List* (2000) of the 570 most common word families
- Dilin Liu's list of most common idioms (2003)

Vocabulary experts agree that academic-bound students who acquire the words on the West and Coxhead lists will know more than 90 percent of the words they will encounter in academic texts (Nation, 2000). Furthermore, research studies have shown that repeated exposure to new words, and application of new vocabulary in writing and speech, increase the chances that students will acquire the target words (N. Schmitt, Nation, Laufer).

From Reading to Writing stresses vocabulary acquisition by providing opportunities for students to encounter, study, and use new words in each of these sections of a chapter or unit:

- Pre-Reading vocabulary activities
- Reading
- Post-Reading vocabulary review
- From Reading to Writing bridge section

Writing Resources

A full complement of appendices serve as resources for student writers. These include a Grammar Reference; a Punctuation and Capitalization section; an Editing Symbols chart, which presents commonly used editing marks, and an alphabetized word list of Target Vocabulary, organized by unit. Additionally, an online e-rater lets students submit their compositions and receive prompt, individualized feedback.

References

Coxhead, A. (2000). "A New Academic Word List." *TESOL Quarterly*, 34(2), 213–38.

Laufer, B. (2003). "Vocabulary Acquisition in a Second Language: Do Learners Really Acquire Most Vocabulary by Reading?" *Canadian Modern Language Review* 59, 4: 565–585.

Liu, Dilin. (2003). "The Most Frequently Used Spoken American English Idioms: A Corpus Analysis and Its Implications." *TESOL Quarterly* 37, 671–700.

Mlynarcyzk, Rebecca. (1993). "Conversations of the Mind: A Study of the Reading/Writing Journals of Bilingual College Students." Diss. New York U, *DAI* 54, 4004A.

Nation, I. S. P. (2001). *Learning Vocabulary in Another Language*. Cambridge: Cambridge University Press.

Schmitt, N. (2000). *Vocabulary in Language Teaching*. Cambridge: Cambridge University Press.

Schmitt, N. & McCarthy, M. (Eds.). (1997). *Vocabulary: Description, Acquisition, and Pedagogy*. Cambridge: Cambridge University Press.

Spack, Ruth. (1993). "Student Meets Text, Text Meets Student: Finding a Way into Academic Discourse." *Reading in the Composition Classroom: Second Language Perspectives*. Joan G. Carson and Ilona Leki (Eds.). Boston: Heinle, 183–96.

Scope and Sequence

Unit		Reading	Reading Skills	Verb Tense Used	Writing Skills	Writing Assignment
1	All in the Family	Chapter 1 *Good Things Come in Fours*	Identifying main ideas	Simple present	Writing complete sentences	Write sentences about families.
		Chapter 2 *Stay-at-Home Dads*			• Using correct paragraph format • Writing compound sentences	Write a paragraph about an interesting relative or friend.
2	Time to Eat	Chapter 3 *Pizza around the World*	Identifying supporting sentences	• Simple present • Simple past of *be*	Writing topic sentences	Write a paragraph about your favorite food or a popular food in your country.
		Chapter 4 *Rachael Ray: Celebrity Chef*		• Simple present • Simple past	Developing a paragraph with supporting sentences	Write a paragraph about the best cook you know or about your favorite celebrity.
3	Overcoming Difficulties	Chapter 5 *Ray Charles*	Recognizing examples	Simple past	• Using examples • Writing a concluding sentence	Write a paragraph about something you are good at or something that is difficult for you.
		Chapter 6 *Whoopi Goldberg*		Simple past	Using main and dependent clauses	Write a paragraph about a person you admire or the kind of work that person does.

Unit		Reading	Reading Skills	Verb Tense Used	Writing Skills	Writing Assignment
4	Places Near and Far	Chapter 7 *An Anniversary to Remember*	Recognizing time order in a narrative	Simple past	• Using description in a narrative • Using the simple past	Write a narrative paragraph about a trip or a memorable experience.
		Chapter 8 *Seattle: A Great Place to Live*			Using time clauses with *before* and *after*	Write a descriptive paragraph about your hometown or favorite city.
5	Keeping Up with Technology	Chapter 9 *Sorry, You've Got Mail*	Understanding pronoun references	• Simple present • Simple past	• Writing a unified paragraph • Using commas	Write a paragraph about the advantages or disadvantages of a kind of technology.
		Chapter 10 *Using YouTube*		Multiple	• Organizing by order of importance • Using connectors	Write a paragraph about the advantages of a kind of technology or of using the Internet.
6	In Business and at Work	Chapter 11 *The Success of Starbucks*	Skimming	• Simple past • Past continuous	Using examples as supporting details	Write a paragraph about a successful business or one you want to start.
		Chapter 12 *Happiness at Work*			• Avoiding sentence fragments • Avoiding run-on sentences	Write a paragraph about a job you enjoy doing now or a job you want to have someday.

(continued)

Unit		Reading	Reading Skills	Verb Tense Used	Writing Skills	Writing Assignment
7	Music	Chapter 13 *A Gift of Music*	Making inferences	Simple past	Using adverbs to show time	Write a paragraph about a kind of music or a hobby you became interested in.
		Chapter 14 *Music and Language*		• Simple present • Simple past	Taking notes for a summary	Write a summary of a reading.
8	Education	Chapter 15 *From a Distance*	Recognizing facts and opinions	• Simple present • Modals	Using *in order to* and *so that*	Write an opinion paragraph about education.
		Chapter 16 *A Healthy Education*		Simple present	• Writing a cause paragraph or an effect paragraph • Using logical connectors to show cause and effect	Write a cause or effect paragraph about students missing class.

UNIT ONE

All in the Family

Good Things Come in Fours

*In this chapter
you will:*

• read about a
  very busy family

• learn to identify
  the main idea of
  a paragraph

• write sentences
  with subjects
  and verbs

PRE-READING

Discussion

Discuss the questions in pairs or small groups.

1. The woman in the photo just had quadruplets (four babies born at the same time). Do you know any families with twins, triplets, or quadruplets?
2. What are some things people have to do to take care of babies?
3. Do you think taking care of babies is hard work? Why or why not?
4. In your country, do most families have only one or two children, or more? Do grandparents, aunts, or uncles usually help?

Vocabulary

A. Read the sentences. Match the boldfaced words with the definitions in the box.

_c_ 1. Debbie and Don got married last week. The **couple** plans to live in Baltimore.

_____ 2. They seem to be very much in love. All their friends **expect** they'll get married.

_____ 3. Quadruplets are very **rare**. Not many women give birth to four babies at the same time.

_____ 4. It is a big **challenge** to take care of four new babies.

> a. not happening very often
> b. think that something will happen
> c. two people who are married or in a romantic relationship
> d. something difficult that you need skill and ability to do

B. Read the sentences. Match the boldfaced words with the definitions in the box.

_____ 1. My cousin Rhoda is my favorite **relative**.

_____ 2. My husband took the children to a movie. The house is quiet, and I'm happy to be home **alone**.

_____ 3. New parents often ask their baby's doctor for **advice**. They ask a lot of questions about how to take care of their child.

_____ 4. If we all **cooperate**, we can clean the house in a few hours.

> a. not with other people
> b. a member of your family
> c. work together to do something
> d. ideas that help someone decide what to do

Good Things Come in Fours

1   In the United States, people celebrate Mother's Day on the second Sunday in May. Many mothers receive flowers and presents. One young mother named Melissa Green got her special Mother's Day presents early. She didn't get just one present. She got four. Two days before Mother's Day, Melissa gave birth to quadruplets. All four of the babies were boys, and all four were healthy. Melissa and her husband, Christopher, named their new sons Jason, David, Mark, and Matthew. They faced many challenges and a lot of joy with their large family.

2   Melissa and Christopher Green always wanted a big family. They just never **expected** to have one so fast. They were already parents. The **couple** has five-year-old twin daughters named Cathy and Lisa. On the morning of May 10, the Greens were a family of four. By the end of the day, they were a family of eight!

3   The Greens were surprised when they learned Melissa was going to have quadruplets. During her doctor's appointment in December, Melissa had a sonogram.[1] The doctor pointed to Baby A, Baby B, Baby C, and Baby D in the picture on the screen. A couple never expects to have four babies at the same time. Quadruplets are very **rare**. They happen only once in every 9,000 births.

4   Melissa and the babies are home from the hospital now, and the Greens are very busy. They are happy, but their lives have changed a lot. Melissa and Christopher remember when the twins were born five years ago. Taking care of Cathy and Lisa was hard work—but what is it like to have four babies in the house? Melissa says, "Taking care of four babies is a huge **challenge**!" It takes about an hour and a half to feed the four babies. After that, the babies sleep, but only for a few hours. Then the whole thing starts again. While the babies are sleeping, Melissa and Christopher try to eat, take showers, shop, do the laundry,[2] and spend time with their daughters. When it's possible, one parent takes a nap[3] while the babies are asleep. The Greens need a lot of energy to take care of all their children, but they are ready for the challenge.

5   The Greens are lucky to be getting a lot of help from their friends and **relatives**. Christopher is staying home for a few weeks, but when he goes back to work, Melissa will not be **alone** with the children. Melissa's best friend lives right next door, and she comes over almost every day. The children's grandparents live in their neighborhood. Christopher's aunt lives nearby, too. She is a pediatrician,[4] and she gives the couple **advice** about taking care of the babies. Cathy and Lisa are helping with their new brothers, too. When all the babies are hungry at the same time, the girls help feed them. Taking care of four babies is a big job. But when everyone **cooperates**, it can even be fun!

[1]**sonogram:** an image that shows a baby before he or she is born

[2]**laundry:** clothes that have just been washed or need to be washed

[3]**take a nap:** sleep a little during the day

[4]**pediatrician:** a doctor who treats children

Identifying Main Ideas

Read each question. Circle the letter of the best answer.

1. What is the reading about?
   a. People celebrate Mother's Day in May.
   b. Having quadruplets is rare.
   c. The Greens are happy to have quadruplets.

2. What is the most important idea in paragraph 4?
   a. The babies are home from the hospital.
   b. Melissa and Christopher don't sleep very much.
   c. The family works hard to take care of four babies.

3. What is the most important idea in paragraph 5?
   a. Melissa's best friend comes over to help almost every day.
   b. The Greens' friends and family help a lot.
   c. Christopher has relatives nearby.

Identifying Details

Each statement is incorrect. Look at the reading again and correct each statement.

1. The Greens' quadruplets were born in ~~March~~. *May*

2. Melissa and her husband named their new sons Jason, David, Mark, and Martin.

3. Some of the babies were healthy.

4. The Greens already had twin sons.

5. Quadruplets happen only once in every 7,000 births.

6. It takes about three hours to feed the four babies.

7. The Green quadruplets sleep for ten hours.

8. Melissa's best friend lives in a nearby city.

Identifying Main Ideas

It is very important to identify the main idea of a paragraph. Remember that a paragraph is a group of sentences about one main idea. To find the main idea, ask yourself, "What is the most important point that the writer is telling me in this paragraph?" The main idea is usually in the first sentence.

Read this paragraph from "Good Things Come in Fours." The main idea is underlined.

> <u>The Greens were surprised when they learned Melissa was going to have quadruplets.</u> During her doctor's appointment in December, Melissa had a sonogram. The doctor pointed to Baby A, Baby B, Baby C, and Baby D in the picture on the screen. A couple never expects to have four babies at the same time. Quadruplets are very rare. They happen only once in every 9,000 births.

Practice

Read each paragraph and circle the letter of the best main idea.

1.   No one thinks twins can be born in different years, but that's what happened with the Lang twins. On New Year's Eve in 2006, Benjamin Lang, a four-pound boy, was born at 11:59 P.M. He was the last baby born in Miami in that year. Then, just ten minutes later, at 12:09 A.M., the second baby was born. Laura Lang, a five-pound girl, was the city's first baby of 2007. What a happy ending to one year—and a happy start to the next!

   a. The first Lang baby was born at 11:59 P.M.

   b. The Lang twins were born in different years.

   c. Laura was the first baby born in Miami in 2007.

2.   Many people in the United States are waiting until they are older to get married. Today the average age for women to marry is 24. The average age for men is 25 years. Some people want to wait until they are making enough money to start a family. Other people want to finish college and work for a few years before they get married. And others say they just aren't ready for the responsibilities of marriage. They want to travel and have a lot of life experiences before they get married.

    a. Many Americans are marrying at an older age.

    b. Today the average age for women in the United States to marry is 24.

    c. Some people in the United States want to get a job before getting married.

3.   Multiple birth means the birth of more than one child at one time; for example, twins, triplets, quadruplets. Multiple births can happen naturally or because of medical treatments. The most common multiple birth is twins. They naturally happen 1 in 89 births. Multiple births increase from medical treatment. Some women who have trouble having children get medical treatments, like IVF. These treatments cause many more twins, triplets, and quadruplets.

    a. Multiple births are common.

    b. Multiple births happen more with medical treatment.

    c. Multiple births happen naturally or from medical treatments.

FROM READING TO WRITING

Reflecting on the Reading

Discuss the questions in pairs or small groups.

1. Do you think it would be fun to be a twin, a triplet, or a quadruplet? Why or why not?
2. Some people wait until they are older to get married. What do you think is the best age to get married? Explain.
3. The Greens have a big family. What do you think are some advantages (good things) of a big family? What are some disadvantages (difficult things)?

Activating Your Vocabulary

A. Complete the sentences with the words from the box.

advice	challenge	couple	~~rare~~
alone	cooperate	expect	relatives

1. The doctor explained that quadruplets are very _____ rare _____.
   The last quadruplets in our city were born almost 10 years ago.

2. When I had my first child, I asked my mother for _____ about taking care of a baby.

3. My parents still live in my hometown, but most of my other _____ have moved to the city.

4. Does anyone _____ to have quadruplets? It's probably always a huge surprise.

5. It was a _____ to take care of my triplets when they were babies. Now that they are older, it is getting easier.

6. Everyone has to _____ in taking care of the triplets. If we don't work together, we'll all be exhausted.

7. Carl and Mary Jackson just had their sixth child. That's when the _____ decided to buy a bigger house.

8. I don't like to babysit _____. I prefer having a friend join me.

B. Complete the paragraph with five words from Exercise A.

When a (1) _____ has a newborn child, they often need help. It is difficult to raise children (2) _____ because they have so many needs. Grandparents and other (3) _____ can help parents meet the (4) _____. If parents and grandparents can (5) _____, together they will provide children with more love and support.

Writing Sentences with Subjects and Verbs

A **sentence** is a group of words that has a subject, a verb, and expresses a complete thought. A sentence begins with a capital letter and ends with a period, a question mark, or an exclamation point.

EXAMPLES

- **The Greens had four babies.**
- **How did they feel?**
- **They were surprised!**

The **subject** of a sentence tells who or what does something. The subject can be a noun or a pronoun.

EXAMPLE

SUBJECT (NOUN)   SUBJECT (PRONOUN)
- **The Greens** visit the doctor. **They** visit the doctor.

The **verb** usually shows the action, or what the subject does.

EXAMPLE

VERB
- The Greens **work** hard.

Sometimes the verb doesn't show an action. It links the subject with the rest of the sentence.

EXAMPLES

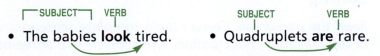

SUBJECT   VERB   SUBJECT   VERB
- The babies **look** tired.   • Quadruplets **are** rare.

In a sentence, the verb must agree with the subject. If the subject is singular, the verb must be singular. If the subject is plural, the verb must be plural.

EXAMPLES

Singular   **Plural**

SUBJECT   VERB   SUBJECT   VERB
- The baby **wants** milk.   • The babies **want** milk.

SUBJECT   VERB   SUBJECT   VERB
- The baby **is** hungry.   • The babies **are** hungry.

Practice

A. Read each group of words. Write S (sentence) or NS (not a sentence) next to each one. Then correct the NS sentences to make them complete.

She works
__NS__ 1. ~~Works~~ very hard.

_____ 2. My sister gives me good advice.

_____ 3. Everyone cooperates.

_____ 4. Four babies a lot of time!

_____ 5. I hungry.

_____ 6. They didn't expect the news.

B. Circle the correct verb form to complete each sentence.

1. I (have / has) two sisters.

2. The father (feed / feeds) his son at night.

3. My favorite relative (live / lives) in Seoul.

4. A big family (have / has) a lot of challenges.

5. My sisters (work / works) in the same office.

6. My best friend (is / are) a wonderful person.

Editing

Read the paragraph. Correct the incomplete sentences, and fix the mistakes in capitalization, punctuation, and subject-verb agreement. There are six mistakes including the example.

are
My husband and I both from large families. he has four brothers, and
and I have two older sisters and two younger brothers. We all live in the
same city, so we get together often Last Sunday, had a big family dinner.
It was for my sister's birthday. Her birthday are on July 16. Everyone
came, and we had a wonderful time! Do you come from a big family, too

WRITING ASSIGNMENT

Write sentences on the topic of families. Follow the steps.

STEP 1 **Get ideas.**

Work in pairs. Ask and answer the questions. If you don't know a word, check your dictionary or ask someone the meaning.

1. Which kind of family do you think is better, a small family, or a large family?
2. What is one challenge for a small family?
3. Why does a large family need to cooperate?
4. How many people are in your family?
5. How much time do you need alone?
6. What is your favorite family activity?
7. What city or town do you think is the best place to raise a family, and why?
8. What do you want to change about your family?

STEP 2 **Write sentences.**

On a piece of paper, write five complete sentences about your family. Use the most interesting information from your conversation with your partner.

STEP 3 **Check your work.**

Read your sentences. Use the Writing Checklist to look for mistakes, and use the editing symbols on page 192 to mark corrections.

> ## Writing Checklist
> ❏ Does every sentence begin with a capital letter?
> ❏ Does every sentence end with a period, a question mark, or an exclamation point?
> ❏ Does every sentence have a subject and a verb?
> ❏ Do the subjects and verbs agree?

STEP 4 **Write a final copy.**

Correct your mistakes. Write a final copy of your sentences and give it to your instructor.

Stay-at-Home Dads

PRE-READING

Discussion

Discuss the questions in pairs or small groups.

1. Look at the picture. What is the man doing?
2. The man in the picture is a father who stays home to take care of his children. Do you know any fathers who stay home to take care of their children?
3. Which words describe a good parent? Check (✔) them.

____ caring	____ patient	____ strict
____ critical	____ responsible	____ strong
____ helpful	____ stressed	____ unfair

Vocabulary

A. Read the boldfaced words and their definitions. Then complete each sentence with the correct word or phrase.

> **adjust:** become familiar with a new situation
>
> **expensive:** something that is expensive costs a lot of money
>
> **quit:** stop doing something
>
> **temporary:** happening for a short period of time

1. My mother _____*quit*_____ her job when I was born. She wanted to stay home with me.

2. This job is _____. I'm only working for the summer.

3. When people move to another country, it is usually difficult for them to _____ to their new home.

4. Many colleges are _____. Parents often start saving for college costs when their children are very young.

B. Read the boldfaced words and their definitions. Then complete each sentence with the correct word or phrase.

> **financial:** related to money
>
> **increase:** rise or become more in amount or number
>
> **practical:** useful and likely to work
>
> **rewarding:** making you feel happy and satisfied

1. The cost of childcare will continue to _____. It was high last year, but it's higher this year.

2. Do you know how to take care of a young child? I need some _____ advice before I start babysitting.

3. Samantha loves being a teacher. She thinks it's a very _____ job.

4. When I started my own business, I needed help with decisions about money. My father gave me _____ advice.

Stay-at-Home Dads

1   Andrea and Matt Brock had their first child four years ago. That's when they made an important decision. Matt remembers the day well. He said, "I'll **quit** my job. I'll stay home and take care of the baby." Andrea was surprised, but she agreed. Matt said, "It's a **temporary** situation. I'll stay home for six months. Then we can hire a babysitter, and I'll go back to work." At first, it was hard for Matt to **adjust** to his new role[1] as a stay-at-home dad. But he enjoyed it, and he decided not to go back to work. Today, four years and three children later, Matt is still home taking care of the children. And he still loves it.

2   Why did the Brocks make this choice? Matt says, "The reason was simple. It was a **financial** decision." Like other couples, the Brocks realized that it did not make sense[2] for both parents to work. They thought about the high cost of childcare, but a full-time babysitter is **expensive**. They also thought about the higher income taxes[3] they paid when they both made money. Andrea said, "We realized that if Matt and I both worked, we made only a few thousand dollars more." Andrea earned more money than Matt did, so that's the reason she decided to keep her job.

3   It is still more common for mothers to stay home and raise the children, but the number of stay-at-home dads is growing every year. In 2003, there were 98,000 stay-at-home dads in the United States. Today there are over 159,000. The number of stay-at-home dads in other countries **increases** every year, too. From Canada and Mexico to Japan and Australia, more and more fathers are staying home to care for their kids.

4   Stay-at-home dads have many challenges. Most say the biggest challenge is loneliness. Stay-at-home dads often feel like outsiders[4] in a world of mothers and children. Matt says, "When I go to the park with my kids, the mothers often don't talk to me." Matt knows only two other stay-at-home dads. They meet once a week to have lunch. "It helps," Matt says, "but I still feel lonely a lot. I wish I knew more men in my situation."

5   In the past, most of the information about parenting was for mothers. That is still true, but today dads can get information, too—especially on the Internet, where there are many websites[5] for stay-at-home dads. The number of books for stay-at-home dads is also growing. One of the most popular books is *The Stay-at-Home Dad Handbook*, which gives **practical** advice to stay-at-home fathers. There is also a convention.[6] Thousands of dads from around the country go to the convention every year to share information and to take classes about parenting. Two of the most popular classes are Child Safety and Kids and the Internet.

6   Most fathers say that raising children isn't easy. Matt says, "It's the hardest job in

---

[1]**role:** the position or job that someone has in a situation or an activity

[2]**make sense:** If it makes sense to do something, it is a reasonable or sensible thing to do.

[3]**income tax:** money you give the government when you earn money

[4]**outsider:** someone who does not belong to a particular group

[5]**website:** a set of pages on the Internet about a particular subject or belonging to a particular organization

[6]**convention:** a large meeting of people who have the same interests

the world, but it's also the most **rewarding**." Most stay-at-home dads agree. They love spending time with their children and watching them grow up. They realize their jobs are very important, and many dads wear T-shirts printed with these words: "Men Who Change Diapers Change the World." They believe that statement is true.

Identifying Main Ideas

Read each question. Circle the letter of the best answer.

1. What is the main idea of the reading?
   a. Most stay-at-home dads find their job challenging but rewarding.
   b. Stay-at-home dads can find information on the Internet.
   c. It is more common for mothers to stay home with the children.

2. What is the biggest challenge for most stay-at-home dads?
   a. feeling alone
   b. learning parenting skills
   c. watching their children grow up

3. What is the main idea of paragraph 3?
   a. There are over 159,000 stay-at-home dads in the United States.
   b. There are stay-at-home fathers in Canada, Mexico, Japan, and Australia.
   c. The number of stay-at-home dads is growing every year.

Identifying Details

Mark the statements **T** *(true) or* **F** *(false). Correct the false statements.*

_F_ 1. When Matt's first child was born, he thought it was ~~easy~~ *hard* to be a stay-at-home dad.

___ 2. Today there are about 98,000 stay-at-home dads in the United States.

___ 3. Matt knows a lot of stay-at-home dads.

___ 4. There is less information about parenting for fathers than for mothers.

___ 5. There are only a few websites for stay-at-home fathers.

Reflecting on the Reading

Discuss the questions in pairs or small groups.

1. Do you think it is a good idea for fathers to stay home and take care of their children? Explain.
2. The article mentions T-shirts that say "Men Who Change Diapers Change the World." Do you agree with this statement? Why or why not?

Activating Your Vocabulary

Complete the sentences with the words from the box.

adjust	financial	practical	~~rewarding~~
expensive	increase	quit	temporary

1. My job as a nurse is hard, but it's very _____rewarding_____.
2. I only plan to live in this apartment for a few months. It is just a _____ place to stay for the summer.
3. It is not easy for me to _____ to time differences when I travel.
4. How do you pay for school? Who gives you _____ help?
5. I wanted to buy that car, but it was too _____. I couldn't afford it.
6. A good nurse needs both education and _____ experience.
7. The number of women who work _____ every year.
8. I _____ my job after I had my baby. I wanted to stay home and take care of her.

Read the model paragraph.

MODEL

Father's Day

Father's Day is an American holiday when children honor their fathers. A woman named Sonora Smart Dodd thought of the idea for Father's Day. Sonora's mother died when she was a young girl. After that, her father, William Smart, took care of her. Sonora wanted to honor her father and other fathers with a celebration. Sonora's father was born in June, so she decided to have the first Father's Day celebration in June. The celebration was on June 19, 1910. In 1972, Father's Day became a national holiday. Today Americans celebrate Father's Day on the third Sunday of June.

WRITING SKILL

Using Correct Paragraph Format

A **paragraph** is a group of sentences about one topic. Paragraphs have a special format. Follow these rules when you write a paragraph:

1. Begin the first line of each paragraph five spaces in from the left margin. This is called *indenting*.
2. Begin each sentence with a capital letter.
3. Do not start each new sentence on a new line.
4. End sentences with a period, question mark, or exclamation point.
5. Include a title.

Practice

Read and correct the sentences. Then use the sentences to write a paragraph in your notebook. Remember to follow the rules of paragraph format.

1. ~~m~~**M**y brother Jim is a stay-at-home dad.

2. he stays at home to take care of his twin daughters

3. they are three years old

4. he is a great father, and he loves his role as a stay-at-home dad

5. jim reads about being a stay-at-home dad on the Internet

6. jim is happy to stay home, but he is busy from morning to night

Writing Compound Sentences

A **compound sentence** is two simple sentences that are joined together. You can join sentences with a **coordinating conjunction** such as *and*, *or*, *but*, or *so*. Compound sentences make your writing more interesting. Always use a comma before the conjunction.

COORDINATING CONJUNCTION	USE	EXAMPLE SENTENCE
and	joins two similar ideas	Alex has twin brothers, **and** he loves them very much.
or	joins two choices	We can make Italian food for lunch, **or** we can order Chinese food.
but	joins two different or opposite ideas	Lee wants to go to California for vacation, **but** his friends want to go to Florida.
so	joins two ideas; the second idea is the result of the first	Tom doesn't like math, **so** he is studying art.

Practice

A. Complete the paragraph. Use and, or, but, or so.

   My older brother's name is Juan. He's a serious person, (**1**) _____ he's fun to be with. He loves to read, (**2**) _____ he buys the newspaper every day. Juan loves to talk, (**3**) _____ he's a good listener, too. I can talk to him about my problems, (**4**) _____ he always gives me good advice. He has a busy schedule, (**5**) _____ he finds time to call me almost every day. If we can't talk on the phone, we send each other e-mail (**6**) _____ we write letters. I'm lucky to have a brother like Juan.

B. Combine each pair of sentences using and, or, but, **or** so. **Compare your sentences with a partner's.**

1. Don likes to take his children to the park. He enjoys taking them to the library, too.

   Don likes to take his children to the park, and he enjoys taking them

   to the library, too.

2. Maria wants to spend more time with her sisters. She is usually too busy.

   _____

   _____

3. Eric wanted to get in touch with his friend. He sent him an instant message.

   _____

   _____

4. Min calls her brother every Saturday. She sends him an e-mail almost every day.

   _____

   _____

5. Ana and Joe want to go out to the movies. They can't find a babysitter to watch their daughter.

   _____

   _____

6. Elsa might wear a dress to the meeting. She might wear a suit.

   _____

   _____

Editing

Read the paragraph. Correct the incomplete sentences, and fix the mistakes in capitalization, punctuation, and compound sentences. There are seven mistakes including the example.

I
~~i~~ grew up in a traditional family. My father went to work every day and my mother stayed at home to take care of the kids. Every night my parents, my sister Ellen, and I had dinner together On Sunday afternoons, we went to my grandmother's house for a big lunch. My aunt Mary, her husband, Tom, and their children came, too. after lunch I played games with my cousins, we all had fun together. I realize the value of family, but I'm raising my children the same way.

WRITING ASSIGNMENT

Write a paragraph. Follow the steps.

STEP 1   **Get ideas.**

Choose a topic for your paragraph. Work in pairs. Complete the sentence, then ask and answer the questions.

❑ **Topic 1:** An interesting relative

❑ **Topic 2:** An interesting friend

My _____'s name is _____.

1. How old is your relative or friend?
2. Where does he or she live?
3. What does this person do? (student, taxi driver, doctor, etc.)
4. What kinds of activities does your relative or friend like to do?

STEP 2   **Write sentences.**

On a piece of paper, write four complete sentences to answer the questions in Step 1. Then write one or two more interesting sentences about your relative or friend. Use a coordinating conjunction in each sentence.

STEP 3   **Write your paragraph.**

Write your paragraph. Begin with the first sentence you wrote in Step 1. Continue with the other sentences you wrote in Step 2.

STEP 4   **Check your work.**

Read your paragraph. Use the Writing Checklist to look for mistakes, and use the editing symbols on page 192 to mark corrections.

Writing Checklist

❑ Did you follow correct paragraph format?

❑ Did you use at least two coordinating conjunctions correctly?

❑ Did you put a comma before coordinating conjunctions?

❑ Does every sentence have a subject and a verb?

STEP 5   **Write a final copy.**

Correct your mistakes. Copy your final paragraph and give it to your instructor.

Time to Eat

Pizza around the World

In this chapter you will:

• read about a popular food

• learn to identify supporting sentences of a paragraph

• write a paragraph with a topic sentence and controlling idea

PRE-READING

Discussion

Discuss the questions in pairs or small groups.

1. Look at the photo. What is the person doing? Do you think this would be a fun job?
2. Do you like pizza? How often do you eat pizza?
3. Do you think that pizza is a healthy food? Why or why not?
4. Making pizza involves baking a pizza pie crust. Do you enjoy baking or cooking? If so, what foods do you like to make?

Vocabulary

Circle the letter of the word or phrase that is closest in meaning to the boldfaced word.

1. I love chocolate. I think it is **delicious**.

   a. expensive   b. fancy   (c.) good-tasting

2. Most of my friends love pizza. More than 75 **percent** say it is their favorite food.

   a. times   b. out of a hundred   c. types

3. Everyone should eat **approximately** 4½ cups of fruits and vegetables every day. Some days I eat a little less, and other days I eat more.

   a. about   b. mostly   c. at least

4. My cooking class was very hard at the beginning, but it is **gradually** getting easier.

   a. finally   b. slowly   c. always

5. There is a **strange** smell in the kitchen. I think we need to clean out the refrigerator.

   a. unusual   b. new   c. surprising

6. Don't eat those mushrooms. They're **poisonous**, and you will get sick.

   a. old   b. dirty   c. harmful

7. Tea is an **international** drink. People all over the world drink it.

   a. in more than one country   b. easily prepared   c. in one country

8. Sugar is the main **ingredient** in candy.

   a. color   b. thing used to make a particular food   c. thing that helps sell a food

Pizza around the World

1   Do you like pizza? If you are like most people, the answer is yes. In fact, pizza is one of the most popular foods in the world. Every year people around the world eat **approximately** 30 billion (30,000,000,000) pizzas. That's a lot of pizza! Ninety-three **percent** of Americans eat pizza at least once a month.

2   Pizza is big business, too. In fact, pizza is a $30 billion per year business. People in the United States spend a lot of money on pizza—more than $22 billion a year. There are over 70,000 pizzerias, or restaurants that make and serve pizza, in the United States. Many other types of restaurants and grocery stores sell pizza, too.

3   A pizza usually has three main parts. On the bottom, there is a round piece of bread dough.[1] On top of the dough, there is tomato sauce and cheese. The final part is the toppings. In other words, pizza is really a meal on a plate of bread.

4   Pizza is not a new food. It developed **gradually** over thousands of years. The ancient Greeks, Romans, and Egyptians ate flat, round bread baked with different toppings. People in Naples, Italy, made something that was like pizza about 500 years ago. They baked round, flat bread on hot stones. Then they put olive oil and spices on top. In the early 1500s, Europeans went to South America. People in South America ate tomatoes, and Europeans brought this fruit back from the New World. But for hundreds of years, Europeans thought tomatoes were **poisonous**, and they weren't interested in eating them. Finally, in the early 1700s, some people in Naples, Italy, started eating tomatoes and discovered that they tasted good on baked bread.

5   Who invented the first pizza? No one knows for sure. Raffaele Esposito made one of the first modern pizzas. Mr. Esposito was a baker in Naples. In 1889, he made a pizza to honor Queen Margherita. It was a special pizza. The **ingredients** were the colors of the Italian flag. Esposito used red tomatoes, green basil leaves, and white cheese. The queen was very happy. She thought it was **delicious**. Esposito named this pizza "the Margherita." The Margherita is still a very popular kind of pizza.

6   Americans and Italians love pizza, and so do millions of people all over the world. Pizza is truly an **international** food. It is easy to change the way pizza tastes. People in different countries just add their favorite toppings. Some of them may sound **strange**, but here are some examples: In Brazil, people like green peas on their pizzas. Australians like shrimp and pineapple. Japanese add corn and squid.[2] Costa Ricans use coconut. Pepperoni is the favorite topping in the United States and the United Kingdom.

7   Today there is pizza in outer space, too. In 2001, Pizza Hut, one of the largest chain pizza restaurants, delivered the first pizza to people at the International Space Station. The pizza went in a rocket.[3] The space pizza had a crust, tomato sauce, and cheese, and it was topped with salami![4]

[1]**dough:** a mixture of flour and water ready to be baked

[2]**squid:** a sea creature with a soft body and ten legs
[3]**rocket:** a machine used to carry something into space
[4]**salami:** a type of sausage that you eat in small, thin slices

Identifying Main Ideas

Read each question. Circle the letter of the best answer.

1. What is the main idea of the reading?
   a. Pizza is a meal on a plate of bread.
   b. Pizza is one of the most popular foods in the world.
   c. Raffaele Esposito invented a special pizza for a queen.

2. What is the main idea of paragraph 4?
   a. The ancient Greeks, Romans, and Egyptians ate flat, round bread baked with different toppings.
   b. Pizza developed gradually over a long time.
   c. For hundreds of years, Europeans thought tomatoes were poisonous.

3. What is the main idea of paragraph 6?
   a. Pepperoni is the number one pizza topping in the United States.
   b. You can change the way pizza tastes.
   c. People all over the world love pizza.

Identifying Details

Look at the reading again and match the time periods with the information.

INFORMATION

_c_ 1. Europeans brought tomatoes back to Europe

____ 2. Raffaele Esposito made one of the first modern pizzas

____ 3. The ancient Greeks, Romans, and Egyptians ate flat, round bread

____ 4. Pizza Hut delivered the first pizza to space

____ 5. People in Naples, Italy, made something similar to pizza

____ 6. People in Naples started eating tomatoes and put them on their baked bread

TIME PERIOD

a. thousands of years ago.

b. 500 years ago.

c. in the early 1500s.

d. in the early 1700s.

e. in 1889.

f. in 2001.

Identifying Supporting Sentences

A well-written paragraph has a main idea and **supporting sentences**. These sentences explain the main idea and give information such as *who, what, where, when, how,* and *why.*

    Read the paragraph. The main idea is underlined. Look at the supporting sentences that follow it, which show *who, why, where,* and *when.*

EXAMPLE

<u>Rice is one of the world's most important foods</u>. Almost three billion people all over the world eat rice. It is the most — **WHO**
important food for people in China and India. Why is it so popular? First, it can grow anywhere, even on hills and — **WHY**
mountains. Indeed, rice is grown in many continents, including China, India, Indonesia, and the United States. Rice is also — **WHERE**
popular because it is easy to cook and store. Rice has been popular for a long time. For example, people have grown it in — **WHEN**
Africa for 3,500 years and in Asia for over 10,000 years.

Practice

A. *Read paragraph 3 on page 26 again. Underline the sentence that gives the main idea.*

B. *Read each main idea and the sentences below it. Check (✔) any sentences that do not support the main idea.*

  1. Chocolate is a very popular food.

     ____ **a.** Many people eat chocolate candy, chocolate cakes, and chocolate ice cream.

     ____ **b.** They eat chocolate hot or cold, in boxes, bottles, or cups.

     ____ **c.** Chocolate is made from the seeds of the cacao tree.

     ____ **d.** The average American eats approximately 12 pounds of chocolate a year.

2. Today we use cacao beans to make chocolate, but many years ago, people in Central and South America used cacao beans as money.

_____ a. For example, a tomato cost one cacao bean, and a turkey cost 90 beans.

_____ b. Some cacao farmers clear sections of the rain forest for their farms.

_____ c. People paid 30 beans for a small rabbit and 80 beans for a piece of cloth.

_____ d. Cacao trees provide food and shelter for many dwellers of the rain forest.

3. Cacoa (chocolate) has been used in Mexico and Central and South America for over three thousand years.

_____ a. Chocolate was found in jars in Oaxaco, Mexico, from around 1200 C.E.

_____ b. Before the 1700s, Europeans had never heard of chocolate.

_____ c. The Maya civilization was drinking it around 400 C.E.

_____ d. The Aztecs drank chocolate in the form of a bitter, spicy drink in the fourteenth, fifteenth, and sixteenth centuries.

FROM READING TO WRITING

Reflecting on the Reading

Discuss the questions in pairs or small groups.

1. Pizza is an international food. What other examples of international foods can you think of?
2. Do you like to try foods from different countries? Why or why not?

Activating Your Vocabulary

Complete the sentences with the words from the box.

approximately	gradually	international	poisonous
delicious	ingredient	~~percent~~	strange

1. Fifty _____*percent*_____ of the students are from Japan. The rest are from Korea and China.

2. I am not a very good cook. But I am taking cooking classes, and I am _____ getting better.

3. This is the most _____ pizza I've ever eaten.

4. Cheese is a basic _____ in pizza.

5. Please make sure the cat doesn't eat the leaves on that plant. They are _____, and she will get sick.

6. There is a _____ smell coming from the basement. Something down there must be bad.

7. Ice cream is an _____ food. People all over the world eat it.

8. I'm not sure exactly how many apples we need to make three pies. I think we need _____ 15.

WRITING

Read the model paragraph.

MODEL

A Very Popular Food

Pho is the most popular food in Vietnam. Pho is a kind of beef noodle soup. The Vietnamese usually eat pho for breakfast, but many people have it for lunch or dinner, too. The main ingredients in pho are broth (a clear soup), beef, and noodles. Sometimes chicken, pork, or shrimp is used instead of beef. Some people make pho at home, but most prefer to eat their favorite food at small soup shops. Pho was first served in the capital of Hanoi about a hundred years ago, and now it is enjoyed throughout the country.

WRITING SKILL

Writing Topic Sentences

A paragraph is a group of sentences about one main idea. The sentence that states the main idea is called the **topic sentence**. It is the most important sentence in a paragraph. The topic sentence is often, but not always, the first sentence of a paragraph. A topic sentence has two parts.

the topic: the subject of the paragraph

the controlling idea: the most important idea about the topic

EXAMPLES

TOPIC ─── CONTROLLING IDEA ───
- Pho   is the most popular food in Vietnam.

TOPIC ─── CONTROLLING IDEA ───
- Pizza   developed gradually over thousands of years.

Practice

A. Read the topic sentences. In each sentence, circle the topic and underline the controlling idea.

1. Gusto's Pizzeria serves the best pizza in town.

2. Rice is the most important food in my country.

3. The food at my college is terrible.

4. Carrots are a healthy snack.

5. People in Turkey drink a lot of tea.

6. My grandmother is the best cook in our family.

7. Breakfast is the most important meal of the day.

8. Chocolate has a long and interesting history.

B. Read each paragraph. Circle the letter of the best topic sentence.

1. _____. First, vegetables have many of the vitamins you need to keep your body working well. For example, dark green vegetables like spinach and yellow vegetables like carrots have vitamin C. Vegetables like broccoli and sweet potatoes are high in fiber. Finally, many scientists believe that eating some vegetables can help fight illness. If you eat vegetables every day, you'll have better health.

   a. There is a lot of vitamin C in dark green and yellow vegetables.
   b. Vegetables taste delicious, especially when they are fresh.
   c. Vegetables are good for your health.

2. _____. People in the Andes Mountains of South America first grew potatoes over 7,000 years ago. When the Spanish arrived in Peru in the 1500s, they were very interested in this vegetable. They thought it was strange but delicious. The Europeans traveling to and from South America brought potatoes home with them. People in Spain started eating and growing potatoes soon after this, and then the rest of Europe learned about this food.

   a. Potatoes have a long and interesting history.
   b. Potatoes are one of my favorite foods.
   c. The first potato farmers were South American.

Editing

Read the paragraph. Fix the mistakes in capitalization, punctuation, and use of coordinating conjunctions. There are six mistakes including the example.

My Favorite Food

P
~~p~~izza is my favorite food. I eat it three or four times a week. I often eat pizza for lunch or dinner and sometimes I eat cold pizza for breakfast. I like to try different combinations of toppings, or my favorite kind of pizza is mushroom and double cheese. when I go to a new city, one of the first things i do is try the pizza there. I've had lots of great pizzas all around the country, so my favorite is still from the pizzeria right in my own neighborhood.

WRITING ASSIGNMENT

Write a paragraph. Follow the steps.

STEP 1   Get ideas.

Choose a topic for your paragraph. Work in pairs. Ask and answer the questions about your topic.

❑ **Topic 1:** Your favorite food

❑ **Topic 2:** A popular food in your country

1. What is the name of the food?
2. What ingredients are in the food?
3. When do you/people eat it?
4. Where do you/people eat it?
5. Why do you/people like it?

STEP 2   Organize your ideas.

Write a topic sentence for your paragraph.

Topic 1: _____

EXAMPLES

- Paella is one of my favorite foods.
- Hamburgers are my favorite food.

Topic 2: _____

EXAMPLES

- Sushi is a very popular food in my country.
- Sandwiches are a popular food in my country.

STEP 3   Write your paragraph.

Start your paragraph with your topic sentence. Then follow with sentences that answer the questions in Step 1.

STEP 4   Check your work.

Read your paragraph. Use the Writing Checklist to look for mistakes, and use the editing symbols on page 192 to mark corrections.

Writing Checklist

❏ Did you use correct paragraph format?

❏ Did you begin your paragraph with a topic sentence?

❏ Did you use at least one coordinating conjunction?

❏ Did you include some of the new vocabulary you learned in this chapter?

❏ Does your topic sentence include a controlling idea?

STEP 5 Write a final copy.

Correct your mistakes. Copy your final paragraph and give it to your instructor.

Rachael Ray: Celebrity Chef

PRE-READING

Discussion

Discuss the questions in pairs or small groups.

1. Look at the photo of Rachael Ray, a famous chef. Chefs usually cook in restaurants. But today many chefs cook on television. What do you know about Rachael Ray or other chefs on TV?
2. Are cooking shows popular in your country? Why do you think they are or are not?
3. Do you like to cook? Tell why or why not.
4. Do you think the culinary (cooking) profession is a good field to work in? Why or why not?

Vocabulary

A. Read the sentences. Match the boldfaced words with the definitions in the box.

_b_ 1. I baked my first cake the other day. I used my mother's **recipe**.

____ 2. People of my grandparents' **generation** don't like to eat frozen food.

____ 3. There is a **celebrity** chef at the party. I love to meet famous people, and I hope I can talk to him.

____ 4. We watched a film about food in Asia. There were more than 100 people in the **audience**.

> a. all the people in a society or family who are about the same age
> b. a set of instructions that tell you how to cook something
> c. the people watching or listening to a movie, concert, TV show, etc.
> d. a famous person, especially in the entertainment business

B. Read the sentences. Match the boldfaced words with the definitions in the box.

____ 1. Her new cookbook was a big **hit**. Everyone loved it.

____ 2. I'm usually hungry when I get home from school, so I have a **snack** a few hours before dinner.

____ 3. I do not want to **influence** your decision. If you want to have pizza at your birthday party, you should have it.

____ 4. I am a chef by **profession**. I went to cooking school for two years.

> a. a job that you need special education and training for
> b. a movie, book, song, show, etc., that is very successful
> c. a small amount of food that you eat between meals
> d. try to change what someone does or thinks

Rachael Ray: Celebrity Chef

1   In the past, most people learned to cook from their mothers and grandmothers. They often used family **recipes** that were passed down from **generation** to generation. People gave each other recipes, and they read cookbooks. Now people are learning how to cook in a new way. They are watching chefs, or professional cooks, on television. These TV chefs teach their **audiences** how to make everything from gourmet[1] meals to simple dinners. The cooks on television are called **celebrity** chefs. One of the most popular celebrity chefs is Rachael Ray. Why do so many people love to watch Rachael Ray cook? She makes cooking look fun and easy.

2   Today cooking shows are more popular than ever. In fact, you can watch cooking shows twenty-four hours a day, seven days a week. People in over 80 million homes around the world are watching them every day! The **audience** is not just homemakers. Almost half the viewers are men, and people of all ages are watching. Steve Manning, a college student, says, "My friends and I are big fans[2] of cooking shows. If we have a class when one of our favorite shows is on, we record the show and watch it later. No one wants to miss Rachael Ray."

3   Rachael Ray wasn't always a celebrity chef, but she always loved food and cooking. Preparing food and eating meals together were very important in her family. As a child, Rachael Ray enjoyed helping her mother and grandfather in the kitchen. Later, she worked in restaurants and grocery stores. She taught cooking classes in Albany, New York, where her specialty[3] was making meals quickly. She showed her students how to make fast, healthy dishes using simple ingredients. In 1998 Ray wrote her first cookbook, called *30-Minute Meals*. The book was a big **hit**. It sold over 10,000 copies in the first few months. Then, in 2001, Ray started cooking on the Food Network on television.

4   Rachael Ray's most famous show is also called *30-Minute Meals*. On this program, she shows how to make a three-course meal in half an hour or less. Ray helps millions of people learn to use everyday ingredients to make easy and delicious meals. *30-Minute Meals* is one of the Food Network's most successful programs.

5   Rachael Ray now has several shows. One is called *$40 a Day*. On this show, Ray goes to different cities looking for the best food at the best prices. She tries to eat three meals and a **snack** for only $40. On another program, *Inside Dish*, Ray visits the kitchens of rich and famous people. Her newest show is called *Tasty Travels*. Can you guess what this show is about? On *Tasty Travels*, Ray gives advice about where to find the world's most delicious food. Rachael Ray is probably the most watched cook in the history of television.

6   Today many young people are interested in becoming chefs, and celebrity chefs like Rachael Ray often **influence** their decision.

(continued)

----

[1]**gourmet:** someone who enjoys and knows a lot about good-quality food and drink

[2]**fan:** someone who likes a particular person very much

[3]**specialty:** a subject that you know a lot about or an activity that you are skilled at doing

Every year, more young people are going to cooking schools. California Culinary Academy is a famous cooking school in the United States. Nancy Seryfert works at the school and says, "Being a chef now is like being a rock star."[4] Tim Ryan of the CCA, says, "More young people than ever are interested in the **profession**. And perhaps more interesting—and important—so are their parents."

[4] **rock star:** a famous rock and roll musician

Identifying Main Ideas

Read each question. Circle the letter of the best answer.

1. What is the main idea of the reading?
   a. Rachael Ray has worked in restaurants, in grocery stores, and on TV.
   b. Rachael Ray's most famous show is called *30-Minute Meals*.
   c. Rachael Ray is one of the most popular celebrity chefs on television.

2. What is the main idea of paragraph 2?
   a. The most popular TV cooking shows are on the Food Network.
   b. Steve Manning is like many other college students: He loves to watch cooking shows.
   c. People in over 80 million homes around the world watch cooking shows.

3. What is the purpose of paragraph 3?
   a. to tell what foods Rachael Ray's family likes
   b. to give background on how Rachael Ray became a chef
   c. to encourage people to go to cooking school

Identifying Details

Look at the reading again and write the topic sentence of the paragraph in which each supporting sentence below appears.

1. Almost half the viewers are men, and people of all ages are watching.
   Topic sentence: *Today cooking shows are more popular than ever.*

2. She taught cooking classes in Albany, New York, where her specialty was making meals quickly.
   Topic sentence: _____

   _____

3. In 1998, Ray wrote her first cookbook, called *30-Minute Meals*.

   Topic sentence: _____

   _____

4. On this program, she shows how to make a three-course meal in half an hour or less.

   Topic sentence: _____

   _____

5. On another program, *Inside Dish*, Ray visits the kitchens of rich and famous people.

   Topic sentence: _____

   _____

6. Every year, more young people are going to cooking schools.

   Topic sentence: _____

   _____

FROM READING TO WRITING

Reflecting on the Reading

Discuss the questions in pairs or small groups.

1. How do people usually learn to cook in your country?
2. Would you like to go to cooking school? Explain.
3. Chefs aren't the only TV celebrities. Who are some other TV celebrities you know? What are they famous for?

Activating Your Vocabulary

Complete the paragraph with the words from the box.

audience	~~celebrity~~	hit	recipe	profession

My favorite (1) _____celebrity_____ chef is Rachael Ray, and she's a big (2) _____ with my whole family, too. I especially like it when she presents a quick (3) _____ for dinner. I'm a police officer, and most people in my (4) _____ don't have a lot of time to cook. Rachael Ray saves me a lot of time in the kitchen. I'll probably be in her TV (5) _____ for a long time to come.

Read the model paragraph.

MODEL

My Favorite Cook

———— TOPIC SENTENCE ————   ———— SUPPORTING SENTENCES ————

My mother is a wonderful cook. She learned to cook as a young girl by helping my grandmother in the kitchen. Her specialty is Italian food. Everyone in our family loves her delicious pasta dishes such as spaghetti and lasagna. Many of my mother's best recipes came from my grandmother. My mother also enjoys watching cooking shows on television and trying the new recipes she sees on her favorite shows. My mother cooks a big dinner for our family every Saturday night, and every month she invites all of our relatives for a big Sunday dinner. She spends about three days preparing all the food for the dinner. All of my relatives and I agree that my mother is the best cook in the whole family.

WRITING SKILL

Developing a Paragraph with Supporting Sentences

You have learned that a good paragraph has two parts: a **topic sentence**, which states the main idea, and **supporting sentences**, which explain the topic sentence. Supporting sentences give examples, facts, and reasons. When you write a paragraph, ask yourself questions about the main idea, such as *who*, *what*, *where*, *when*, *how*, and *why*. This can help you think of supporting sentences to include in your paragraph.

Practice

A. **Look again at the model paragraph on this page. Write answers to the questions below about the topic sentence. Copy the supporting sentences from the paragraph. Then compare your answers with a partner's.**

1. **Who** does she cook for?

   My mother cooks a big dinner for our family every Saturday night, and every month she invites all of our relatives for a big Sunday dinner.

2. **What** is her specialty?

   _____

   _____

3. **Where** did she get her recipe?

_____

_____

4. **When** did she learn to cook?

_____

_____

5. **How** did she learn to cook?

_____

_____

B. Read each topic sentence. Circle the letter of the sentence that does NOT support the main idea.

1. Breakfast is the most important meal of the day.

    a. Breakfast gives your body the energy it needs to start the day.

    b. A good breakfast helps you think clearly, solve problems, and remember things.

    c. Many families enjoy eating together.

    d. Children who eat breakfast do better in school, and adults who eat breakfast perform better at work.

2. I had a dinner party for my friend's birthday, and it was terrible.

    a. I cooked the chicken for too long, so it was dry.

    b. I gave my friend a CD for her birthday.

    c. Some people didn't get any salad because I didn't make enough.

    d. I burned the birthday cake, and we couldn't eat it.

3. Many people believe that garlic is good for your health.

    a. Scientists are proving that garlic can fight some kinds of cancer.

    b. Doctors think garlic can help prevent heart disease, too.

    c. Fresh garlic has a strong smell and is difficult to peel.

    d. Garlic can also help you feel better when you have a cold or sore throat.

Editing

Read the paragraph. Fix the mistakes in capitalization, punctuation, and use of coordinating conjunctions. There are six mistakes including the example.

My Favorite Chef

Masaharu Morimoto is my favorite celebrity chef, or I watch him on TV often. he was born in Hiroshima, Japan, where he learned how to make sushi and other Japanese dishes. When he was 30 years old, Morimoto moved to New York City? In New York, Morimoto learned many other kinds of cooking. Today he still uses traditional Japanese flavors in his dishes, so he also uses Chinese spices and simple Italian ingredients. finally, he is also influenced by French cooking. Morimoto is truly a chef with an international flavor.

WRITING ASSIGNMENT

Write a paragraph. Follow the steps.

STEP 1 **Get ideas.**

Choose a topic for your paragraph. Work in pairs. Ask and answer the questions about your topic.

❏ **Topic 1:** The best cook you know

1. Where did he or she learn to cook?
2. How did this person learn to cook?
3. When does he or she cook?
4. What kinds of food does he or she cook?
5. Why do people like what he or she cooks?

❏ **Topic 2:** Your favorite celebrity

1. Why is this celebrity famous?
2. How did this person become a celebrity?
3. What do you like about him or her?
4. Where do you see this celebrity?

STEP 2   Organize your ideas.

A. Write a topic sentence for your paragraph.

_____

EXAMPLE

- My uncle is the best cook I know.

B. On a piece of paper, make an outline like the one below. Choose ideas from Step 1 that support the topic sentence.

Topic sentence:

Supporting sentence:

Supporting sentence:

Supporting sentence:

Supporting sentence:

STEP 3   Write your paragraph.

Write your paragraph. Follow the outline in Step 2.

STEP 4   Check your work.

Read your paragraph. Use the Writing Checklist to look for mistakes, and use the editing symbols on page 192 to mark corrections.

Writing Checklist

❑ Did you use correct paragraph format?

❑ Does your paragraph begin with a topic sentence?

❑ Does your topic sentence include a controlling idea?

❑ Does your paragraph include at least three supporting sentences?

❑ Do the supporting sentences give more information about the main idea?

STEP 5   Write a final copy.

Correct your mistakes. Copy your final paragraph and give it to your instructor.

UNIT THREE

Overcoming Difficulties

Ray Charles

PRE-READING

Discussion

Discuss the questions in pairs or small groups.

1. What kinds of music do you listen to? Check (✔) your answers. Use your dictionary to look up any new vocabulary.

   ____ classical   ____ rock and roll   ____ jazz   ____ hip-hop

   ____ Latin   ____ folk/country   ____ pop   ____ reggae

   ____ other: _____

2. Who are some great musicians? Where are they from?

3. Look at the photo of Ray Charles. What do you know about this singer and musician?

Vocabulary

A. Read the sentences. Match the boldfaced words with the definitions in the box.

__d__ 1. It's not easy to have a **career** in music. That's why many musicians have other jobs, too.

____ 2. Some children can play the piano very well **in spite of** their small hands.

____ 3. A person who is blind (unable to see) has a **disability**. People who are deaf (unable to hear) and people who cannot walk also have disabilities.

____ 4. Musicians are more **aware** of sounds and music than most people.

---

a. knowing that something is happening or is true
b. without being affected or prevented by a problem
c. a physical or mental condition that makes it difficult for a person to do something that most other people can do
d. a job that you know a lot about and that you do for a long time

---

B. Read the sentences. Match the boldfaced words with the definitions in the box.

____ 1. Children need parents. Children cannot **survive** all alone.

____ 2. Some people **take advantage of** those who are not strong or who don't know something. That is not right.

____ 3. Musicians and artists **create** new music and works of art.

____ 4. I **admire** people who can write good music. They have my respect.

---

a. feel great respect and liking for someone or something
b. use a person in a way that is not fair
c. continue to live when life is difficult or after an accident or an illness
d. make something new

Ray Charles

1   Ray Charles was a very important American singer and musician. During his long **career**, he made many great records and won many awards.[1] For example, he received 12 Grammy Awards because other musicians respected his work. Ray Charles had a great career **in spite of** serious problems in his life.

2   Ray had a very difficult childhood. He grew up in Florida during the Great Depression, a very hard time in the 1930s. Many Americans had no jobs then, and many people were poor. Ray's family was especially poor. Ray said, "Even compared to other blacks . . . we were on the bottom of the ladder looking up at everyone else. Nothing below us except the ground." During his early years, he had many other problems, too. For example, his father was absent most of the time. Then, when Ray was five years old, he saw his younger brother drown.[2] Soon after that, Ray began to go blind, and by the age of seven, he could not see anything at all.

3   Ray had to learn how to live with his **disability**. His mother helped him meet that challenge by never letting him feel sorry for himself. For example, she taught him how to become independent by finding things and doing things for himself. When he was seven, Ray went to live at a school for the deaf and blind. Ray learned to read and compose music in Braille[3] at this school and to play a variety of musical instruments.

4   Soon music became the most important thing in Ray's life. His blindness made him very **aware** of sounds. Because he could not see, he listened more carefully than other people. He loved all kinds of music, and he often stayed up late at night listening to the radio. He felt a need for music. He once said, "I was born with music inside me. It was a necessity for me, like food and water."

5   Ray's career in music began early, and it was not easy. When he was 15 years old, his mother died. Ray then decided to leave school. He began playing the piano for small bands, and he traveled all over Florida. Because life was hard for a young blind man, Ray had to be smart to **survive**. For instance, he often asked people to pay him in one-dollar bills. That way, he could count all the money and no one could **take advantage of** him.

6   At age 16, Ray made a good career decision and moved to Seattle, Washington. There he met another talented young musician named Quincy Jones. Jones taught Ray how to write and arrange music. Ray later played in nightclubs in Seattle, and he began to **create** his own kind of music. It was a mix of gospel music[4] and the blues.[5] People called it *soul music*. Many people liked it, so they bought Ray's records. His audiences grew larger and larger, and he became a celebrity. During the 1950s and '60s, he recorded many hit songs and became rich.

---

[1]**award:** a prize given to someone for doing something special
[2]**drown:** die from being underwater too long
[3]**Braille:** a form of printing with raised round marks that blind people can read by touching

[4]**gospel music:** music traditionally sung by African-Americans in church
[5]**the blues:** a style of music from the African-American culture of the southern United States, usually slow and sad

7   The last years of Ray's life were some of the best of his career. Ray's music from the 1950s and '60s became popular again in the 1990s. Young people started listening to his earlier songs. Other musicians **admired** him, and many asked for the chance to work with him.

8   Ray Charles, who died in 2004, had a big influence on American music in spite of a serious disability. Many people today continue to enjoy and respect his work.

Identifying Main Ideas

Read each question. Circle the letter of the best answer.

1. What is the main idea of the reading?
   a. Ray Charles was a great American singer and musician.
   b. Ray Charles's disability did not stop him from having a great career in music.
   c. Ray Charles had a sad, difficult life with many serious problems.

2. What is the main idea of paragraph 2?
   a. Ray Charles had a difficult childhood.
   b. Ray Charles grew up during the Great Depression.
   c. Ray Charles watched his brother drown.

3. Why did Ray Charles become famous and respected?
   a. He learned to read Braille.
   b. He created a new kind of music.
   c. He survived a difficult childhood.

Identifying Details

Look at the reading again and match the events in Ray Charles's life with the time periods.

LIFE EVENTS		TIME PERIODS
_b_	1. He saw his younger brother drown	a. during the 1950s and 1960s.
____	2. He went completely blind	
____	3. He lost his mother	b. at the age of five.
____	4. He went to work in Seattle, Washington,	c. when he was seven years old.
____	5. He created a new kind of music	d. in the 1990s.
____	6. His music became popular again	e. at the age of 15.
		f. when he was 16.

Recognizing Examples

READING SKILL

Writers often use **examples** to explain their ideas. Examples are bits of information that explain or describe a point. They can include facts, dates, numbers, and descriptions of events. An example sometimes begins with the transition words *For example* or *For instance*.

EXAMPLE

⌐TRANSITION WORDS⌐

- Ray Charles played many musical instruments. **For example**, he played the piano.

Practice

Look back at the reading on pages 48–49. Find each idea below. Then find a sentence in that paragraph that gives an example of the idea. Write the sentence.

1. Ray Charles won many awards for his music. (paragraph 1)

   For example, he won 12 Grammy Awards because other musicians respected his work.

2. Ray had a difficult childhood. (paragraph 2)

   _____

   _____

3. Ray's mother helped him. (paragraph 3)

   _____

   _____

4. Ray had to be smart to survive. (paragraph 5)

   _____

   _____

FROM READING TO WRITING

Reflecting on the Reading

Discuss the questions in pairs or small groups.

1. Many musicians admired Ray Charles. Who do you admire and why?
2. People sometimes tried to take advantage of Ray. Do people ever take advantage of you? Explain.
3. Ray Charles's mother helped him learn to live with his blindness. Who helps you with difficulties in your life? Give examples of one or two people and how they help you.

Activating Your Vocabulary

Which sentence is closest in meaning to the one with the boldfaced word or phrase? Circle the letter.

1. During the Great Depression, the government had to **create** jobs.
   a. The government had to make new jobs for people.
   b. The government had to take away people's jobs.

2. Some people tried to **take advantage of** Ray.
   a. They did not treat him fairly.
   b. They paid him a lot of money.

3. Many people **admired** Ray Charles's musical talents.
   a. They respected him because he was a great musician.
   b. They were surprised that he was a great musician.

4. People who are blind or who can't walk have a **disability**.
   a. They have no abilities.
   b. They can't do things that most people can do.

5. Were you **aware** of Ray Charles's work in music?
   a. Did you like his work?
   b. Did you know about his work?

6. Quincy Jones helped Ray with his **career**.
   a. Jones helped Ray with the job Ray did for a long time.
   b. Jones helped Ray with his friends.

7. Ray learned to **survive** after his blindness.
   a. He learned to understand his problems.
   b. He learned to continue with his life when it was difficult.

8. Ray was successful **in spite of** his problems.
   a. He was not stopped by his problems.
   b. He talked to people about his problems.

Read the model paragraph.

MODEL

My Special Talent

I am good at public speaking. I like to talk in front of large groups of people. For example, I like to give speeches in class. I don't feel nervous. I became aware of my ability in third grade. I liked to learn poems and say them in front of my class. Everybody clapped for me, and I liked that. Later, my teachers gave me important parts in school plays. For instance, in sixth grade, I was Dorothy in *The Wizard of Oz*. In high school, I won a speaking contest. I really enjoy public speaking, and I want to learn more about it.

**WRITING
SKILL**

Using Examples

You can use **examples** to support the main idea of a paragraph. They help to make your main idea clear to the reader. You can introduce an example with these transition words followed by a comma:

- For example,
- For instance,

These transition words have the same meaning. Use them to introduce a complete sentence, not just words. (Remember, a complete sentence has a subject and a verb, and expresses a complete thought.)

EXAMPLE   SUBJECT + VERB

- I like to talk in front of large groups of people. **For example**, <u>I like</u> to give speeches in class.

Practice

A. *Read the model paragraph again. Underline the two sentences that show examples. Circle the transition words.*

B. *Each sentence has a punctuation error or is incomplete. Look at the reading on pages 48–49 again and correct each sentence.*

1. Ray's mother helped him. For example, be independent.

   Ray's mother helped him. For example, she taught him to

   be independent.

2. Ray won many awards. For instance, 12 Grammy Awards.

_____

_____

3. Bad things happened to Ray, for example, his brother drowned.

_____

_____

4. As a boy, Ray loved listening to music, on the radio, for instance.

_____

_____

5. Ray learned to play several instruments. For example, the piano and the clarinet.

_____

_____

6. Ray had many hit songs in his career. "Georgia on My Mind," for example.

_____

_____

WRITING SKILL

Writing a Concluding Sentence

A paragraph ends with a **concluding sentence**. The concluding sentence summarizes the main idea found in the topic sentence. Sometimes a concluding sentence repeats words or ideas from the topic sentence.

EXAMPLE

> Ray Charles had a successful career in spite of being blind. He learned to play many different instruments, and he became a respected musician. He wrote and sang his own songs, and he led big bands. He made great records for more than 50 years. **Ray Charles did not let his blindness stop him from having a great career in music.**

Sometimes a concluding sentence states the writer's opinion about the topic.

EXAMPLE

> Ray Charles overcame many problems in his life. He grew up poor, and he could not depend on his father. He lost his eyesight by the age of seven. Then, when he was a teenager, his mother died, and he had to depend on himself. He managed to be independent and have a great career in spite of being blind. **I think Ray Charles was a brave man.**

Practice

A. Look at the model paragraph on page 52. Copy the topic sentence and the concluding sentence. Then circle the words that repeat the ideas in the two sentences.

Topic sentence: _____

Concluding sentence: _____

B. Read each paragraph. Copy the best concluding sentence on the lines below.

1. I am good at making clothes. I like to make clothes for myself and my family. For example, I made my wedding dress, and I make dresses for my little girls. I learned to sew from my mother, and I still use her old sewing machine. _____

   _____

   a. You can save money by making clothes.
   b. I enjoy the time I spend making clothes.
   c. I am planning to buy a new sewing machine.

2. It is difficult for me to read maps. Sometimes I get into trouble because I can't understand a map. For example, when I first came here, I couldn't read the subway map. I got lost, and I was in the subway for three hours. I couldn't ask for directions in English. Now I'm good at asking for directions. _____

   _____

   a. I often need directions when I drive.
   b. However, I am still bad at reading maps.
   c. I had my cell phone, but it didn't work in the subway.

Editing

Read the paragraph. Correct the incomplete sentences and fix the mistakes in capitalization, punctuation, and use of coordinating conjunctions. There are seven mistakes including the example.

My Problem

It is difficult for me to understand English. ~~w~~Ⱳhen people speak to me, I usually do not understand. For example: I don't understand salespeople in stores. In my country, I learned a lot of grammar, but listening to English very difficult. became aware of this problem when I came to the United States I did not understand the people in the airport. This problem is very hard for me and sometimes I feel like a child. Now I am trying hard to improve my listening ability. For example, taking classes and listening to the radio and TV. I hope I will understand more because I need English to survive.

WRITING ASSIGNMENT

Write a paragraph. Follow the steps.

STEP 1   **Get ideas.**

Choose a topic for your paragraph. Work in pairs. Ask and answer the questions about your topic.

❑ **Topic 1:** Something you are good at

1. What are you good at?
2. What example of this ability can you give?
3. When did you become aware of this ability?
4. Did anyone tell you that you had this ability or help you with it?
5. How do you use this ability?

❑ **Topic 2:** Something that is difficult for you

1. What is difficult for you?
2. What example of this difficulty can you give?
3. When did you become aware of this problem?
4. How does this problem affect you?
5. What are you doing about this problem?

STEP 2   **Organize your ideas.**

A. Complete a topic sentence for your paragraph.

Topic 1: I am good at _____.

EXAMPLES
- I am good at math.
- I am good at playing the piano.

Topic 2: It is difficult for me to _____.

EXAMPLE

- **It is difficult for me to remember people's names.**

B. On a piece of paper, make an outline like the one below. Choose ideas from Step 1 that support the topic sentence. Add a concluding sentence.

Topic sentence:

Supporting sentence:

Supporting sentence:

Supporting sentence:

Supporting sentence:

Concluding sentence:

STEP 3   Write your paragraph.

Write your paragraph. Follow the outline in Step 2.

STEP 4   Check your work.

Read your paragraph. Use the writing checklist to look for mistakes, and use the editing symbols on page 192 to mark corrections.

Writing Checklist

❑ Did you use correct paragraph format?

❑ Did you write complete sentences, with subjects and verbs?

❑ Does your paragraph begin with a topic sentence?

❑ Do you have at least one sentence with an example?

❑ Does your paragraph have a concluding sentence?

STEP 5   Write a final copy.

Correct your mistakes. Copy your final paragraph and give it to your instructor.

Whoopi Goldberg

PRE-READING

Discussion

Discuss the questions in pairs or small groups.

1. Look at the photo of Whoopi Goldberg. What do you know about her from TV or movies?
2. How did you feel about school when you were a child? How did you feel about reading?
3. What kinds of things do you read every day? Check (✔) your answers.

    ____ dictionaries   ____ books   ____ food labels

    ____ magazines   ____ menus   ____ web pages

    ____ newspapers   ____ signs   ____ maps

    ____ other: _____

Vocabulary

Circle the letter of the word or phrase that is closest in meaning to the boldfaced word or phrase.

1. Dyslexia is a disability that affects the **brain**. It affects how a person thinks and learns.
   a. part of the head
   b. part of the stomach
   c. part of the lungs

2. Some children have trouble learning to read. With hard work, many **overcome** their problem and become good readers.
   a. identify
   b. control
   c. forget

3. Do you ever feel **confused** in school? Are there things that are not clear to you?
   a. not able to understand
   b. out of place
   c. upset

4. Learning a new language is not often easy. It can be a real **struggle**.
   a. time to learn
   b. goal
   c. long, hard fight

5. Some words don't **make sense** if they are not spelled correctly.
   a. fit
   b. have a clear meaning
   c. have prefixes

6. Some people are **lazy**. They do not want to work hard.
   a. not liking to work
   b. learning easily
   c. late

7. I get **upset** if I study hard for a test but get a bad grade.
   a. loud or strong
   b. sad or unhappy
   c. ready

8. Teachers **encourage** children with reading problems. They tell them to keep trying, and they try to give them hope.
   a. help
   b. ignore
   c. find

Whoopi Goldberg

1   Most actors learn their lines by reading a script.[1] But what about an actor who cannot read? What if all the words and letters just look mixed up on the page? That is what happens to people with dyslexia. Dyslexia is a learning disability that makes the **brain** mix up the order of letters and words. Dyslexia makes it hard for people to read and write. They may know a word on one page and not know it on the next page. Often they have trouble spelling, especially with vowels. Whoopi Goldberg has dyslexia. She is a famous American actress and comedian[2] who has acted in over 140 movies and TV shows. Whoopi **overcame** her disability through a lot of hard work.

2   Growing up in New York, Whoopi didn't know she had dyslexia. She knew only that school was hard. Reading especially was very challenging for her, and she often felt **confused**. She says, "I knew I wasn't stupid. My mother told me that. Everybody told me I wasn't dumb. If you read to me, I could tell you everything that you read. They didn't know what my problem was. They knew I wasn't **lazy**, but what was it?" Whoopi often felt **upset** about her problems in school. Finally, she quit school and moved to Los Angeles.

3   One day, a friend wrote a sentence on a blackboard. Whoopi said to him, "You know, I can't read that. It doesn't **make** any **sense** to me." He told Whoopi that she might have dyslexia. He told her to write the letters she saw under his letters. He taught her to read by matching what she saw to the letters of the alphabet. Whoopi practiced this new way of reading. Reading was still a **struggle** for her, but gradually, she made progress.

4   At first, life in Los Angeles was hard, too. Whoopi wanted to find work in Hollywood movies, but it was not easy. She worked at a variety of temporary jobs to survive. After a long time, she got her first job as a comedian because she had a talent[3] for acting and making people laugh. Later, Whoopi got work in movies, plays, and TV shows, and she won many awards for her work. She never let her disability stop her.

5   Whoopi is not the only celebrity with dyslexia. Other famous actors, such as Tom Cruise, Salma Hayek, and Orlando Bloom, all work hard to overcome this learning disability. For example, Tom Cruise learns all of his lines by listening to a recording. Even famous artists such as Leonardo da Vinci and Pablo Picasso were dyslexic. Da Vinci wrote his notes about art backwards from left to right because he had a disability. Picasso often painted things upside down or out of order— as he saw them. However, most people who have dyslexia are not famous. About 10 percent of the people in the United States have it.

6   Today, Whoopi speaks openly about her disability to **encourage** children who have

(continued)

---

[1]**script:** the written form of a speech, play, television or radio show, or movie
[2]**comedian:** a person whose job is telling jokes and funny stories

[3]**talent:** ability

learning disabilities. She also asks people to be careful how they speak to children with such problems. She has said, "You can never change the effect that the words *dumb* and *stupid* have on young people." In addition, Whoopi works with other actors to help homeless people. She overcame a big problem in her own life, and she believes other people can do the same.

Excerpt from the Academy of Achievement interview with Whoopi Goldberg

Identifying Main Ideas

Read each question. Circle the letter of the best answer.

1. What is the main idea of the reading?
   a. Some movie stars have problems with dyslexia.
   b. Whoopi Goldberg has worked hard to overcome dyslexia.
   c. Dyslexia is a disability that makes it hard to read and write.

2. What is the main idea of paragraph 4?
   a. Whoopi succeeded in her career in spite of her disability.
   b. Whoopi worked at a lot of different jobs over time.
   c. Life in Los Angeles was hard for Whoopi, but she eventually found success.

3. What is the purpose of paragraph 5?
   a. to give examples of other famous people with dyslexia
   b. to tell about Pablo Picasso's paintings
   c. to tell how many people have dyslexia

Identifying Details

Each statement is incorrect. Look at the reading again and correct the statements.

1. Whoopi always knew she wasn't ~~smart~~ *stupid*.

2. Whoopi finished high school.

3. Her teachers said Whoopi might have dyslexia.

4. Tom Cruise learns his lines by reading them over and over again.

5. About one percent of people in the United States have dyslexia.

6. Whoopi Goldberg works with other actors to help people without jobs.

Reflecting on the Reading

Discuss the questions in pairs or small groups.

1. Reading is difficult for Whoopi because she has dyslexia. Reading can also be difficult for people learning English. Why?
2. Whoopi encourages others to overcome their problems. Do you encourage your friends to try to do things that are hard? Does anyone encourage you? Explain.
3. Whoopi dreamed of working in Hollywood movies, and she made her dream come true. Do you have a dream? Explain.

Activating Your Vocabulary

Complete the paragraphs with the words from the boxes. You will not use all of the words.

encourage	~~make sense~~	overcome
struggle	upset	

School is often very challenging for children with learning disabilities. Some subjects do not (1) ___make sense___, and doing homework is a (2) _____. It is natural for children to feel (3) _____ about their problems with school. They need help to (4) _____ their problems.

brain	confused	encourage	lazy	overcome

Jonah is in the first grade. He is learning to read, but it isn't easy. He often feels (5) _____. His mother and father (6) _____ him to work harder. Jonah is trying hard. He isn't (7) _____. He has dyslexia, and it affects his (8) _____.

Read the model paragraph.

Temple Grandin

I admire Temple Grandin because she overcame a disability. Temple has autism. Because autism affects the brain, people with this problem usually struggle to communicate. Temple did not talk until she was almost four years old. In school, she had fights with other students because they laughed at her. Today, she has a Ph.D. in animal science. She thinks animals are a lot like people with autism. She understands animals well, so she feels comfortable with them. She writes books and goes on TV to teach people about animals. I respect Temple Grandin because she is a strong person.

Using Main and Dependent Clauses

When you give reasons for something, use *because* in a sentence. A sentence with *because* has two parts:

A main clause. The main clause is a complete sentence.

A dependent clause. The dependent clause has a subject and verb, but it does not express a complete thought. It is not a complete sentence and must always be attached to a main clause.

EXAMPLE

        ━━━━━━ MAIN CLAUSE ━━━━━━━━┐ ┌━━━━ DEPENDENT CLAUSE ━━━━

- It's hard for autistic children to make friends because they don't talk much.

The dependent clause can come before or after the main clause. The meaning is the same. When the dependent clause comes *first*, use a comma.

EXAMPLE

      ━━ DEPENDENT CLAUSE ━━┐ ┌━━━━━━━ MAIN CLAUSE ━━━━━━━

- Because they don't talk much, it's hard for autistic children to make friends.

Practice

A. Look again at the model paragraph. Find two sentences with because. For each, circle the main clause and underline the dependent clause.

B. Combine each pair of sentences with because. Write each sentence in two ways: with the main clause first and last.

1. Reading is hard for Whoopi Goldberg. She has dyslexia.
   Reading is hard for Whoopi Goldberg because she has dyslexia.
   Because she has dyslexia, reading is hard for Whoopi Goldberg.

2. Whoopi felt confused in school. She could not read.
   _____

   _____

3. She moved to Los Angeles. She wanted to be in movies.
   _____

   _____

4. She worked at a variety of jobs. It was hard to get work in movies.
   _____

   _____

5. She talks about her disability. She wants to encourage other people with problems.
   _____

   _____

C. Complete the sentences.

1. Because __*I didn't have time*__, I didn't __*eat breakfast today*__
   _____

2. I am learning English because _____
   _____

3. I like _____ because _____
   _____

4. I want to _____ because _____
   _____

5. Because _____, my friends don't _____
   _____

Editing

Read the paragraph. Correct the incomplete sentences, and fix the mistakes in capitalization, punctuation, and use of coordinating-conjunctions. There are eight mistakes including the example.

My Father

I admire my ~~F~~*f*ather. Because he is responsible and hard-working. He works the second shift in a mattress factory. it was a temporary job, so they asked him to stay, because he a good worker. Now he has a regular job with benefits. My father always works when he's at home, too. He is not lazy. He's good at fixing things. For example: when a friend has a problem with his car, he asks my father for help. I admire my father because works hard and helps people.

WRITING ASSIGNMENT

Write a paragraph. Follow the steps.

STEP 1 Get ideas.

A. Choose a topic for your paragraph. Work in pairs. Ask and answer questions about your topic.

❑ **Topic 1:** Someone you admire

❑ **Topic 2:** The kind of work the person you admire does

B. Make a list of the person's qualities or actions that you admire. Use a chart like this one.

PERSON I ADMIRE: MY GRANDMOTHER	
1. brave	She was brave to come to this country as a young girl.
2. worked hard	She worked hard to raise a family.

STEP 2 **Organize your ideas.**

A. Complete a topic sentence for your paragraph.

Topic 1: I admire _____.

EXAMPLE

- I admire Temple Grandin because she overcame a disability.

Topic 2: I value _____.

EXAMPLE

- I value my father because he listens to me when I have a problem.

B. On a piece of paper, make an outline. Look back at your ideas in Step 1. Write supporting sentences for your topic sentence. Add a concluding sentence.

STEP 3 **Write your paragraph.**

Write your paragraph. Follow the outline you made in Step 2.

STEP 4 **Check your work.**

Read your paragraph. Use the writing checklist to look for mistakes, and use the editing symbols on page 192 to mark corrections.

Writing Checklist

❑ Did you use correct paragraph format?

❑ Did you begin your paragraph with a topic sentence?

❑ Do you have at least one sentence with an example?

❑ Did you use *because* correctly?

❑ Does your paragraph have a concluding sentence?

STEP 5 **Write a final copy.**

Correct your mistakes. Copy your final paragraph and give it to your instructor.

Places Near and Far

An Anniversary to Remember

PRE-READING

Discussion

Discuss the questions in pairs or small groups.

1. What do you know about Canada?
2. Look at the photo. Have you ever taken a long train trip? If so, did you enjoy it? If not, would you like to? Explain.
3. What is your favorite way to travel? Why?
4. If you could travel throughout one country, which country would you visit? What would you see there?

Vocabulary

A. Read the sentences. Match the boldfaced words with the definitions in the box.

___c___ 1. My parents have been married for 25 years. They celebrated their **anniversary** with a big party.

_____ 2. We'll get to the Atlanta airport at 7:00. We'll **board** the plane for Seattle at 8:30.

_____ 3. We stayed in a **luxurious** hotel with big rooms, three wonderful restaurants, and two swimming pools.

_____ 4. The room was **elegant**, with chandeliers and fancy furniture.

a. very expensive, beautiful, and comfortable
b. showing grace and beauty
c. the date when people celebrate something important that happened on the same day in a previous year
d. get on an airplane, train, ship, etc.

B. Read the sentences. Match the boldfaced words with the definitions in the box.

_____ 1. We want to **explore** the city and see its interesting buildings.

_____ 2. Look at the **magnificent** view of the mountains. We need to take a picture!

_____ 3. The **scenery** is very beautiful in this part of Canada, especially the rivers and waterfalls.

_____ 4. I like to **keep in touch** with my friends by e-mail.

a. very good because of being very big, beautiful, etc.
b. continue to speak or write to someone who does not live near you
c. the natural things you can see in a place, such as mountains, forests, etc.
d. travel around an area to find out what it is like

An Anniversary to Remember

1   Ian and Beth Parker lived near Toronto, Canada. Their fifth wedding **anniversary** was in a few weeks. They wanted to do something special to celebrate. One day, Beth read an article about a train ride called *Romance by Rail*. The ride was a three-day, 4,452-kilometer (2,765-mile) trip across Canada. The trip sounded different from the usual vacations Beth and Ian took to a museum or the beach. They could experience the beauty of the Canadian countryside on a **luxurious** train. So Ian bought tickets for their anniversary journey. The Parkers were ready to take a relaxing and romantic[1] train trip across Canada.

2   The couple **boarded** the train at Toronto's Union Station on Tuesday morning. An attendant[2] showed them their deluxe[3] room. There were *two* bathrooms, a big bed, comfortable chairs, and huge windows. There were also beautiful fresh flowers on the table and fancy chocolates on the bed pillows. After the train left Toronto, it traveled west past **magnificent** lakes, rivers, and forests. The Parkers watched all this wonderful **scenery** from their room. Next, they went to the **elegant** dining car for a delicious lunch. They soon discovered that traveling by train is a great way to meet people. First, the Parkers met Hector and Cecilia Gómez, who were teachers from Mexico. Then Beth and Ian met two Japanese students, Masa Sato and Kiku

Tanaka. This was their first train trip across Canada, and they were very excited about seeing the country.

3   In the evening, the Parkers went to the Park Car, the last car on the train. It had a glass dome[4] that offered wonderful views in all directions. "I'll never forget watching the sunset in the evening and the stars at night," Beth said. "That's when I understood the magic of train travel."

4   The next day was Beth and Ian's anniversary. After they exchanged gifts, they met their new friends Hector and Cecilia for breakfast in the dining car. In the afternoon, the scenery changed. The train began its long journey across the huge Canadian prairies. From the windows, Beth and Ian watched elk, moose, wolves, and deer running across the prairies. It was a relaxing day. The Parkers were happy being together and enjoying the scenery.

5   Thursday was the most exciting day of the trip. In the afternoon, the train stopped for an hour in the small mountain town of Jasper. Ian remembers that stop very well. "When I got off the train," he said, "I saw four huge elk standing right in the station." The Parkers **explored** the town's shops and art galleries. Later, Beth and Ian spent the afternoon in the Park Car. They both thought the prettiest part of the trip was the ride from Jasper to Vancouver. That's when the train crossed through the magnificent Canadian Rocky Mountains. It was a clear day, so they saw Mount Robson, the highest peak[5] in the

[1]**romantic:** beautiful in a way that strongly affects your emotions; making you have feelings of love for someone
[2]**attendant:** someone whose job it is to take care of customers on an airplane, a train, etc.
[3]**deluxe:** better and more expensive than other things of the same type

[4]**dome:** a rounded roof on a building or a room
[5]**peak:** the pointed top of a mountain

Rockies. Everyone agreed that this must be the best way to see the Canadian Rockies.

6   The Parkers were sad when the train finally arrived in Vancouver on Friday morning. Beth and Ian, Hector and Cecilia, and Masa and Kiku exchanged e-mail addresses and promised to **keep in touch**. Their trip was over, but the Parkers will always remember their romantic fifth anniversary train ride. In fact, they've decided they will take the trip again to celebrate their 10th anniversary—and maybe their 50th, too!

Identifying Main Ideas

Read each question. Circle the letter of the best answer.

1. What is the main idea of paragraph 1?
   a. The Parkers usually went to museums or the beach.
   b. The Parkers were ready for a train trip across Canada.
   c. The Parkers bought train tickets.

2. What is the main idea of paragraph 5?
   a. Mount Robson is the highest peak.
   b. Jasper is a small town with shops and art galleries.
   c. Thursday was the most exciting day.

3. What reason for taking a train trip across Canada is NOT in the reading?
   a. It is a wonderful way to see Canada's beautiful scenery.
   b. It is the fastest way to travel from Toronto to Vancouver.
   c. It is a good way to meet people and make new friends.

Identifying Details

Each statement is incorrect. Look at the reading again and correct the statements.

three

1. *Romance by Rail* is a ~~six~~-day trip across Canada on a luxurious train. *three*

2. The train left Union Station on Monday morning.

3. After the train left Toronto, it traveled north past lakes, rivers, and forests.

4. The Parkers met Hector and Cecilia Gómez in the Park Car.

5. Jasper is a big city in the mountains.

6. Mount Robson is the highest peak in the Cascade Mountains.

Recognizing Time Order in a Narrative

The reading on pages 70–71 is a **narrative**. A narrative is a story that often (but not always) tells events in **time order**. **Time-order words** help move the reader from the first event to the next to the last. They include adverbs and phrases:

TIME-ORDER WORDS	
Adverbs	**Prepositional Phrases**
first next later then finally yesterday last year	after the movie at 2:30 in the afternoon on Tuesday

Time-order words may come in different places in a sentence. They often start a sentence. When a time-order word starts a sentence, it is often followed by a comma.

EXAMPLE

- **First**, they took a train to Montreal.
  They took a train to Montreal **first**.

- **At 2:30**, they reached the train station.
  They reached the train station **at 2:30**.

Practice

A. Read the paragraph and circle the six time expressions.

Winter Trip to New York

We arrived at New York's LaGuardia Airport at 2:30. At first we were going to take a taxi. Then we decided to take a bus. We got to Grand Central, New York's famous old train station, at about 3:15. There was a winter light show in the station. There were lights and starry, snowy scenes on the ceiling. We watched the light show for a half hour. After that, we walked slowly through the beautiful building.

B.   Number the events in the order they happened.

_____ 1. The Parkers ate lunch.

_____ 2. The Parkers met Masa and Kiku.

  _1_   3. The train left Toronto.

_____ 4. The Parkers met Hector and Cecilia.

_____ 5. The Parkers watched the scenery from their room.

_____ 6. The Parkers went to the Park Car.

_____ 7. The train traveled west.

C.   Read the paragraph. Underline the ten time expressions.

My Week in Siem Reap

Last year, I spent a week working for the Wheelchair[1] Project in Siem Reap, Cambodia. The Wheelchair Project is an example of _voluntourism_, a new kind of vacation experience. Voluntourism combines traditional travel with volunteer work. Volunteer work is work without pay. I arrived in Siem Reap in the morning. First, I went to a welcome lunch where I met the other volunteers in my group. After that, we visited the famous Angkor Wat Temple, one of the most beautiful buildings in the world. Our work started the next day. We learned how to make special wheelchairs for moving on Cambodian country roads and rice fields. Later, we spent three days making the wheelchairs. On Thursday night, we had a party and presented the wheelchairs to the people who needed them. Finally, on my last day, I took a bike ride around the beautiful countryside of Siem Reap. My week with the Wheelchair Project was one of the best experiences I've ever had.

Statue, Angkor, Cambodia

....

[1]**wheelchair:** a chair with wheels for people who cannot walk

Reflecting on the Reading

Discuss the questions in pairs or small groups.

1. Would you like to take a trip across Canada like the one described in the article? Explain why or why not.
2. Do you like to meet new people? Where do you usually meet new people?

Activating Your Vocabulary

Complete the sentences with the words from the box.

anniversary	elegant	keep in touch	magnificent
~~boarded~~	explore	luxurious	scenery

1. We _____ *boarded* _____ the bus at 5:00, but it didn't leave until 5:30.
2. The _____ in this part of the country is beautiful. You can see mountains, rivers, and forests.
3. Let's _____ the village before we get back on the train.
4. We _____ by e-mail.
5. The views of the mountains are _____.
6. We took a trip on a small but _____ cruise ship. It had comfortable rooms, fine food, and wonderful service.
7. We are going to celebrate our 10th _____ in Spain.
8. The restaurant in the old part of the city was _____. It had stained glass windows and gold tablecloths.

WRITING

Read the model paragraph.

MODEL

City of Hills

When I was 22, I went to San Francisco. It was the most magnificent city I had ever seen. The first thing I saw were the steep hills of Nob Hill and Telegraph Hill. Red cable cars circled up and down the hills. Then I took the Geary bus and rode it as far as it went to Ocean Beach. When I got off, I quickly climbed up to Sutro Heights Park, with its ocean views, and smelled the salty air.

WRITING SKILL

Using Description in a Narrative

A good narrative gives **descriptive details**. It uses adjectives, adverbs, and specific verbs to help the reader to form a picture of the story, or to feel a certain emotion. Look at the example for the model paragraph.

EXAMPLE

ADJECTIVES	ADVERBS
magnificent steep red ocean (views) salty	first then quickly

Practice

Read the paragraph. Circle the adjectives and underline the adverbs.

Next I walked all around the seashore until I came to Baker Beach. From there I saw the Golden Gate Bridge. It was a rusty color. The sun was slowly coming down, so the bridge glowed. Along the beach were bits of green and gray seaweed. A hawk hovered over the beach. It moved very slowly in the wind. At last the sun came down and the sunset was beautiful.

WRITING SKILL

Using the Simple Past

Most narratives are written about events in the past. A verb in the past tense tells about an action that happened in the past. For regular verbs, form the past tense by adding *-ed* to the base verb.

EXAMPLES

- The train travel**ed** west.
- They watch**ed** the scenery.

If a regular verb ends in *-e*, just add *-d*.

EXAMPLES

- The Parkers liv**ed** near Toronto.
- Ian agre**ed** on a train trip.

Change the spelling of irregular verbs to form the past tense.

EXAMPLES

- Ian and Beth **bought** (buy) train tickets.
- It **was** (be) a relaxing day.

Practice

A. Complete the sentences with the past form of the verb in parentheses.

1. I _____ (walk) around Golden Gate Park yesterday.
2. There _____ (be) a rose garden in the park.
3. We _____ (ride) a bus from the park to the Palace of Fine Arts.
4. We _____ (sit) and _____ (rest) on a bench while we looked at the lake and statues.
5. It _____ (start) to rain, but we _____ (stay) where we were.
6. The rain _____ (come) down harder, so we _____ (decide) to take shelter under some statues.
7. After a while, we _____ (go) into a museum nearby until the rain _____ (stop).
8. We _____ (wait) at the bus stop to return home.
9. Several buses _____ (pass) before our bus _____ (arrive).

B. Complete the paragraph with the simple past of the verbs in parentheses.

Last year I _____ (visit) Quebec City, Canada. First, we _____ (walk) near the ramparts, the old city walls. Next, we _____ (take) a tour bus down to the old city, where we _____ (see) a pretty seventeenth century church, Notre-Dame-des-Victoires. Then we _____ (shop) in the old square and _____ (buy) lunch. Last, we _____ (explore) the farmer's market, the Marche du Vieux-Port.

Editing

Read the paragraph. Fix the mistakes in capitalization, punctuation, use of the past tense, and use of time-order words. There are eight mistakes including the example.

    Last year, Carola and Aaron celebrate^d their 20th wedding anniversary with a two-month trip around the world. on June 20, they fly from their home in Mexico City to Washington, D.C. They spent three days in Washington. Before they flew to London, where they enjoy a week of sightseeing. On Friday, they take the Chunnel train to Paris. They stayed in Europe for a few weeks. Next, they took the train to Istanbul and visited many places in Asia. Their last stop in Asia is Tokyo, where they spent five days Finally, they flew back home to Mexico City. It was an anniversary they will never forget.

Write a paragraph. Follow the steps.

STEP 1 **Get ideas.**

Choose a topic for your paragraph. Work in pairs. Ask and answer the questions about your topic.

❑ **Topic 1:** A trip I took

1. When and where did you go on your trip?
2. How did you get there?
3. What interesting things did you do or see?
4. What did you do first?
5. What did you do after that?
6. What was the best or worst part of the trip?

❑ **Topic 2:** A memorable experience

1. What was the experience?
2. When and where did it happen?
3. How did you feel? (excited, scared, sad, etc.)
4. What happened first?
5. What happened next?
6. What did you learn from the experience?

STEP 2 **Organize your ideas.**

A. Write a topic sentence for your paragraph. Include a word or phrase that tells the main idea of the story.

Topic 1: _____

EXAMPLES

- Last summer, I took a wonderful trip to Seoul, Korea.
- I had a fantastic time on my trip to Egypt last winter.

Topic 2: _____

EXAMPLES

- My first day in the United States was exciting.
- I'll never forget the frightening experience I had during a snowstorm last winter.

B. On a piece of paper, make an outline. Look back at your ideas in Step 1. Write supporting sentences for your topic sentence. Add a concluding sentence.

STEP 3   **Write your paragraph.**

Write your paragraph. Follow the outline you made in Step 2.

STEP 4   **Check your work.**

Read your paragraph. Use the Writing Checklist to look for mistakes, and use the editing symbols on page 192 to mark corrections.

Writing Checklist

❑ Did you start the narrative with a topic sentence that tells the main idea?

❑ Did you include supporting sentences that show the main point?

❑ Did you use correct past tense verb forms?

❑ Did you use time expressions to show order?

❑ Did you include a concluding sentence?

STEP 5   **Write a final copy.**

Correct your mistakes. Copy your final paragraph and give it to your instructor.

Seattle: A Great Place to Live

PRE-READING

Discussion

Discuss the questions in pairs or small groups.

1. Look at the photo of Seattle, Washington. It is in the northwest part of the United States. Find this area on a map. What cities, towns, mountains, or bodies of water do you recognize in this area?
2. Would you like to live near water and mountains? Why or why not? Explain your answer.
3. What is your favorite city? Explain your answer.

Vocabulary

A. Read the sentences. Match the boldfaced words with the definitions in the box.

_c_   **1.** My brother has an **opportunity** to attend a college in Seattle.

_____   **2.** I like the **location** of my apartment. It's near many stores.

_____   **3.** There are many advantages to going to a **multicultural** school.

_____   **4.** The city is on an island. It is **surrounded** by water.

> **a.** having something go all around
> **b.** having many different cultures
> **c.** chance
> **d.** place

B. Read the sentences. Match the boldfaced words with the definitions in the box.

_____   **1.** Is it **worth** waiting in such a long line for this movie?

_____   **2.** Canada and Mexico signed a **trade** agreement.

_____   **3.** The view from the top of the mountain is **spectacular**.

_____   **4.** Lowell, Massachusetts, is known for its **diversity**. For example, Puerto Ricans, Vietnamese people, and Cambodians all live there.

> **a.** wonderful or exciting
> **b.** different people and things
> **c.** related to buying and selling
> **d.** good to do

C. Complete the paragraph with words from Exercises A and B.

Seattle is a (1) _____ city. Many different groups of people live there. For example, many Chinese Americans live in the International District. Vietnamese, Filipinos, Laotians, and others also live in this (2)_____. In Seattle there is also plenty of (3) _____ to meet Spanish speakers. Of course, the schools have a lot of (4)_____, with many languages spoken.

Seattle: A Great Place to Live

1   Before you decide where you want to live, check magazines like *Money* and *Forbes*. They make lists of the best cities to live in. In the United States, the following cities have been on these lists: Portland, Oregon; Denver, Colorado; and Pittsburgh, Pennsylvania. Internationally, Vancouver, Canada; Sydney, Australia; Paris; and Hong Kong have been called the best in the world. What makes a city "the best"? Some important features are **location**, weather, jobs, and things to do and see.

2   Seattle, Washington, has been at the top of the list several times. Many people love this city because of its natural beauty. In fact, some people think it is one of the most beautiful cities in the world. Seattle is built on hills and **surrounded** by water and mountains. It is on a small piece of land between Puget Sound[1] and Lake Washington. From the hills, there are **spectacular** views in every direction. To the west are the Olympic Mountains, and to the east are the Cascade Mountains. On a clear day, you can see Mount Rainier, an ice-covered active volcano.

3   The weather in Seattle is another reason people love the city. It's almost never too hot or too cold. People who live there say the summers are wonderful. The daytime temperature is in the 70s, and at night it is in the 50s.

4   Seattle is enjoyable for people who like spending time outside. It has nice weather and a location near both water and mountains, so there are many things to do. You can see people riding bicycles, running, and walking outside all year long. The Cascade and Olympic Mountains and the Pacific Ocean are all close. You can go fishing, hiking, mountain biking, or rock climbing.

5   Seattle is also a good place to live if you like to do things indoors. The city has lots of cultural attractions: excellent museums, wonderful theaters, and great music. One of the most famous attractions is the Pike Place Market. Over 600 farmers, fishermen, flower sellers, and artists sell their products there. This year-round market is more than 100 years old.

6   There are many job **opportunities** in Seattle because it is an important city of **trade** and business. It is a port[2] city, so it is a center for trade with Canada, Mexico, Europe, and Asia. The city is also home to some of the world's largest companies in the computer software, e-commerce,[3] and aerospace[4] industries.

7   Seattle is often called the "Emerald[5] City" because of its many parks. Beautiful green forests are also nearby. The city has other nicknames, too, such as the "Rainy City" because it rains so much in the winter. Seattle is sometimes called "the Gateway to Asia" because it is near the Pacific Ocean.

8   Seattle is a **multicultural** city with a lot of friendly people. It even has festivals that celebrate its **diversity**. The Northwest Folk Life Festival is one of the most popular

---

[1] **Puget Sound:** a body of water that leads to the Pacific Ocean

[2] **port:** a place where ships can load or unload goods
[3] **e-commerce:** the practice of buying and selling things on the Internet
[4] **aerospace:** involving the building of airplanes and space vehicles
[5] **emerald:** bright green like the valuable green stone of the same name

festivals. This multicultural celebration lasts for four days. You can listen to music and watch dance performances from around the world. There is food from many different countries.

9   Almost everyone agrees that Seattle is a great place to live and visit. However, no city is perfect. Seattle has some of the same problems other cities have. One of its biggest problems is traffic. Most of the time, there are so many cars on the roads that it is difficult to get around the city. Even on the weekends, the highways are often crowded. Still, most people who call Seattle home think it is **worth** fighting the traffic to live there.

Identifying Main Ideas

Read each question. Circle the letter of the best answer.

1. What is the main idea of the reading?
   a. Seattle has great weather and beautiful scenery.
   b. There are many job opportunities in Seattle.
   c. Seattle is a wonderful place to live.

2. What is the main idea of paragraph 6?
   a. Seattle is a good place to find a job.
   b. Seattle is a port city.
   c. E-commerce is very important in Seattle.

3. How is Seattle like many other U.S. cities?
   a. It's expensive.
   b. The traffic is terrible.
   c. The weather is perfect.

Identifying Details

Complete the sentences with the correct words from the reading.

1. The Olympic Mountains are to the _____*west*_____ of Seattle.
2. In the summer, the temperature is usually in the _____ during the day and in the _____ at night.
3. Pike Place Market is more than _____ years old.
4. Seattle is important for trade with Canada, Mexico, Europe, and _____ because it is a port city.
5. Seattle is often called the "_____ City" because of its parks and the beautiful green forests around the city.
6. The Northwest Folk Life Festival lasts _____ days.

Reflecting on the Reading

Discuss the questions in pairs or small groups.

1. People who live in Seattle love it for many reasons. What are some things you love about your city or town?
2. According to the reading, Seattle has a problem with traffic. Is that a problem where you live? Explain your answer.
3. The reading states that Seattle is a city with people from many cultures. What are the advantages of living in a multicultural city?

Activating Your Vocabulary

Circle the letter of the word or phrase that is closest in meaning to the boldfaced word.

1. My house is **surrounded** by tall trees.
   a. supported **b.** having something go all around c. drawing a circle

2. The library is in a good **location**. It is near the bus stop, so it's easy to get there.
   a. place b. direction c. building

3. I love to look out of my bedroom window. I have a **spectacular** view of the mountains.
   a. distant b. wonderful c. open

4. The United States has increased **trade** with India. The two countries now exchange many more products.
   a. tourists b. communication c. buying and selling

5. I was glad to have the **opportunity** to visit the wonderful city of Seattle.
   a. advantage b. challenge c. chance

6. London is a city of great **diversity**. There are many different kinds of people there.
   a. different people and things b. sameness c. jobs

7. We live in a **multicultural** neighborhood with people from all over the world.

   a. orderly   **b.** having many different cultures   **c.** having a different climate

8. It's very expensive to live in San Francisco. But people who live there say it's **worth** the expense because it's such a wonderful city.

   a. equal to   **b.** encouraging   **c.** practical

WRITING

Read the model paragraph.

MODEL

The Best of Bangkok

My city, Bangkok, is a wonderful place to visit. Bangkok is located in the central part of Thailand. There are many things to do in Bangkok. For example, you can visit some of the magnificent temples. After you visit the temples, you can go to the royal Grand Palace. Don't forget to see the Pak Khlong Talat, the biggest flower market in the city. The restaurants in Bangkok are wonderful. In addition to Thai food, you can eat French, Italian, Japanese, and Korean meals. Before you leave Bangkok, you should watch kick-boxing, a favorite sport in Thailand. You should also try to see traditional Thai dancing. I'm sure you will enjoy your time in Bangkok.

Using Time Clauses with *before* and *after*

We use *before* and *after* to tell when something happens. *Before* and *after* are often used in **time clauses**.

EXAMPLE

┌── TIME CLAUSE (DEPENDENT) ──┐┌────── MAIN CLAUSE ──────┐
- **Before** you visit a city, find out about the weather there.

A time clause is a **dependent clause**. As you learned in Unit 3, a dependent clause is not a complete sentence by itself. It must always be attached to a **main clause**. The dependent clause can come before or after the main clause.

EXAMPLES

┌──── TIME CLAUSE (DEPENDENT) ────┐┌───── MAIN CLAUSE ─────┐
- **After** you listen to music, you can taste the food.

┌───── MAIN CLAUSE ─────┐┌──── TIME CLAUSE (DEPENDENT) ────┐
- You can taste the food **after** you listen to music.

Remember, when a dependent clause comes first in the sentence, use a comma after it. When the main clause comes first, do not use a comma.

Practice

A. *Combine each pair of sentences with* before *or* after. *Write the combined sentence in two ways: with the time clause first and last.*

1. I washed all my clothes. I packed my suitcase. (before)

   I washed all my clothes before I packed my suitcase.

   Before I packed my suitcase, I washed all my clothes.

2. Julia read a book about Turkey. She went to Istanbul. (before)

   _____

   _____

3. I spent the morning at the museum. I had lunch at a Thai restaurant. (after)

   _____

   _____

4. They went to a kick-boxing match. They left Bangkok. (before)

   _____

   _____

5. I bought a map. I drove to St. Louis. (before)

_____

_____

6. John left his hotel. He went to a London theater. (after)

_____

_____

B. Complete the sentences about yourself. Include a comma where necessary.

1. Yesterday, before I ____brushed my teeth____ , I ____took a shower____ .

2. Before I _____ this morning I _____ .

3. In the afternoon, I usually _____ after I _____ .

4. Before I _____ last night I _____ .

5. I like to _____ after I _____ .

6. I _____ before I _____ .

Editing

Read the paragraph. Fix the mistakes in capitalization, punctuation, and use of time clauses. There are seven mistakes including the example.

Visiting Taos

Taos, New Mexico, is one of my favorite places to visit. Taos is located at the bottom of the Sangre de Cristo Mountains. ~~y~~Y̲ou can enjoy Taos any time of the year. In the winter, you can go skiing and snowboarding In the summer, you can go hiking and enjoy the beautiful scenery. There are things to do indoors, too? Before you leave Taos you should visit some of the wonderful art galleries and museums. My favorite is the Harwood Museum of Art. The paintings in the museum show the multicultural history of Taos. Before you visit Taos. You will understand why it is famous for its beauty and its diversity.

Write a paragraph. Follow the steps.

STEP 1 **Get ideas.**

Choose a topic for your paragraph. Work in pairs. Ask and answer questions about your topic.

❑ **Topic 1:** Your city or hometown

❑ **Topic 2:** Your favorite city

1. What is the name of your hometown / favorite city?
2. Where is it located?
3. When was the last time you visited?
4. What is it famous for?
5. What can you do there?
6. Does it have interesting museums or monuments?
7. How is the food there?

STEP 2 **Organize your ideas.**

A. Write a topic sentence for your paragraph.

Topic: _____

EXAMPLES

- My hometown is San Juan, Puerto Rico.
- San Juan, Puerto Rico, is my hometown.
- Last summer, I visited the great city of Sydney.
- When I was a child, my family went to Osaka.

B. On a piece of paper, make an outline. Look back at your ideas in Step 1. Write supporting sentences for your topic sentence. Use time clauses with *before* and *after*. Add a concluding sentence.

STEP 3   **Write your paragraph.**

Write your paragraph. Follow the outline you made in Step 2. Add time clauses with *before* and *after*.

STEP 4   **Check your work.**

Read your paragraph. Use the Writing Checklist to look for mistakes, and use the editing symbols on page 192 to mark corrections.

Writing Checklist

❑ Did you begin your paragraph with a topic sentence?
❑ Did you include sentences that support your topic?
❑ Did you use at least one time clause?
❑ Did you use correct punctuation in the time clause?
❑ Did you use correct paragraph format?

STEP 5   **Write a final copy.**

Correct your mistakes. Copy your final paragraph and give it to your instructor.

Keeping Up with Technology

Sorry, You've Got Mail

PRE-READING

Discussion

Discuss the questions in pairs or small groups.

1. Which do you receive more: e-mail or letters (snail-mail) from the post office? How many of each do you get in a week?
2. Who sends you snail-mail or e-mail?
3. Are there some kinds of mail or e-mail that you don't like to get? Explain what kinds.
4. E-mail can sometimes give computers viruses. Do you have a computer? Has it ever gotten a virus? What can you do to protect it?

Vocabulary

Read the sentences. Match the boldfaced words with the definitions in the box.

__b__ 1. I like to use **technology** such as my cell phone, my computer, and the Internet.

____ 2. **Communication** is easy with e-mail. You can send information to people quickly.

____ 3. A letter or an e-mail can carry a **message** from one person to another.

____ 4. Many people with things to sell put **advertisements** in newspapers, magazines, on the Internet, and in e-mails.

____ 5. Some e-mail users have a computer **program** to block the e-mail they do not want.

____ 6. E-mail viruses can **spread** fast. They can go quickly from one computer to another.

____ 7. That computer company is famous, so the company's name is **familiar** to most people.

____ 8. I'm having a problem with my computer. I don't know how to **deal with** it.

---

a. a piece of information that you leave for someone when you cannot speak to him or her

b. machines, equipment, and ways of doing things that are based on modern knowledge of science and computers

c. words, pictures, short movies, etc. which try to make people buy a product or use a service

d. the act of speaking or writing to someone and being understood by him or her

e. known well, recognizable

f. pass from one place to another and affect more and more people

g. do something to solve a problem

h. a set of instructions for a computer that makes it do something; a kind of software

---

Sorry, You've Got Mail

1   Bill Gates loves **technology**. He probably likes using e-mail. It makes **communication** easier, both at work and with friends. But Gates probably does not love opening his e-mail. He receives over 4 million **messages** a day. Most of these messages do not come from his friends or co-workers.[1] They are the kinds of e-mail that bring problems: spam, phishing e-mail, and messages with viruses.

2   Spam is e-mail that nobody wants. It comes from people with something to sell, like medicine or land or an idea for making money. The sellers try to find buyers by sending out spam with **advertisements**. They often send thousands of these messages at a time. In fact, 70 percent of all the e-mail on the Internet is spam. That means more than 1 million pieces of spam go out every second! These unwanted messages can create problems for the people who get them. For example, many office workers get more spam than useful e-mail. It can take them a lot of time to delete[2] all those messages. So, many companies use computer **programs** that help block spam.

3   Phishing e-mails are another big problem. These e-mails look as if they come from a **familiar** bank or company, but they really come from criminals.[3] The criminals try to take advantage of e-mail users by sending phishing e-mails with false information. For example, they say that the bank or company has a new website.[4] Then they tell readers to go to the website and type in their bank account or credit card number. When someone does that, the criminals can then try to use the account number. There are now laws and computer programs to help stop phishing, but e-mail users still receive 6.1 billion phishing e-mails every month. They need to read their e-mail very carefully so they won't be fooled.

4   Computer viruses are a serious problem, too. A virus is a program that changes how a computer works. It makes bad things happen to the computer. The worst virus to date was the ILOVEYOU virus. In the spring of 2000, it hit over 45 million computers around the world. When an e-mail user opened a message with this virus, the virus deleted files[5] from his or her computer. Then the virus **spread** from that computer to the computers of friends and co-workers. In the end, it cost businesses over 14 billion dollars. Today, every e-mail user needs to know about computer viruses. There are over 50,000 of them in the world, and a new one is sent almost every 18 seconds.

5   Every e-mail user has to **deal with** spam, phishing, and viruses. In spite of these serious problems, most people still like using e-mail. It makes communication both faster and easier. Even Bill Gates probably prefers 4 million e-mails to 4 million letters or phone calls.

----

[1]**co-worker:** someone who works with you
[2]**delete:** erase a piece of information from a computer's memory
[3]**criminal:** someone who breaks the law
[4]**website:** a set of pages on the Internet about a particular subject or belonging to a particular organization

[5]**file:** information on a computer that is stored under a particular name

Identifying Main Ideas

Read each question. Circle the letter of the best answer.

1. What is the main idea of the reading?
   a. E-mail makes work much easier today.
   b. E-mail viruses are a serious problem.
   c. Some kinds of e-mails cause problems.

2. What is the main idea of paragraph 2?
   a. Nobody likes advertisements.
   b. There are too many advertisements in spam.
   c. Many e-mail users have a problem with spam, or unwanted e-mail.

3. What is the main idea of paragraph 3?
   a. Some e-mails come from criminals.
   b. Phishing e-mails are a problem for many people.
   c. E-mail users need to read their e-mail very carefully.

Identifying Details

Mark the statements T (true) or F (false). Correct the false statements.

                                 million

__F__ 1. Bill Gates gets 4 ~~thousand~~ e-mail messages a day.

_____ 2. Spam usually comes from someone you know.

_____ 3. People send about 1 million spam messages every day.

_____ 4. A virus is a program that changes the way a computer works.

_____ 5. Phishing e-mails are messages with advertisements.

_____ 6. Phishing e-mails come from criminals.

_____ 7. The ILOVEYOU virus only damaged computers in the United States.

_____ 8. Companies buy software to protect their computers from spam.

Understanding Pronoun References

When you read, it is important to see the connections between nouns and **pronouns**. Pronouns take the place of nouns. A pronoun refers to a noun that came before it.

EXAMPLE

• (Bill Gates) loves technology. **He** probably likes using e-mail.

Two kinds of pronouns are subject pronouns and object pronouns.
Subject Pronouns: *I, we, you, he, she, it, they*
Object Pronouns: *me, us, you, him, her, it, them*

Practice

Read the paragraph. Circle each pronoun. Draw an arrow to the noun that it refers to.

Last week when Rafael checked his e-mail, (he) got a strange message. It said that the e-mail was from his bank. The e-mail sender wrote that the bank had lost customers' personal information. As a result, it needed their social security numbers. Rafael deleted the message because he knew it was a phishing e-mail.

FROM READING TO WRITING

Reflecting on the Reading

Discuss the questions in pairs or small groups.

1. Bill Gates probably prefers e-mail to letters or phone calls. Which kind of communication do you prefer? Why?
2. The reading describes three kinds of e-mail problems. Which one do you think is the most serious? Explain.
3. Do you like using new technology? Explain.

Activating Your Vocabulary

Which sentence is closest in meaning to the one with the boldfaced word or phrase? Circle the letter.

1. Many people use new **technology** at work.
   a. They work with new people.
   b. They have new machines and ways of doing things. *(circled)*

2. The news **spread** slowly.
   a. It took time for more people to learn the news.
   b. The news got more and more interesting.

3. Please give her this **message**.
   a. Give her this information from me.
   b. Give her this gift from me.

4. **Communication** is important to people in the business world.
   a. People in the business world must have the newest machines.
   b. People in the business world must speak and write to others.

5. Some e-mail messages have **advertisements**.
   a. Some e-mail messages tell about things for sale.
   b. Some e-mail messages cause harm to people's computers.

6. Be careful opening e-mail if the sender is not **familiar** to you.
   a. Be careful opening e-mail if you do not know the sender.
   b. Be careful opening e-mail if you do not like the sender.

7. All e-mail users have to **deal with** viruses.
   a. All e-mail users must buy viruses.
   b. All e-mail users must know what to do about viruses.

8. I have a new computer **program**.
   a. I have a new part for my computer.
   b. I have new software to use in my computer.

Read the model paragraph.

MODEL

> ### The Camera in My Cell Phone
>
> My cell phone camera has several advantages. It is small, light, and easy to carry. I always have my phone with me, so I don't need to plan to take photos. I am ready to take them at any time. I often take photos when I am with my friends. Then I can send the photos to my friends in text messages. My friends and I do this a lot because it is fun and easy to share photos this way. I can also send photos from my phone to my computer, and then I can save them or print them. For all these reasons, I am happy to have a camera in my cell phone.

WRITING SKILL

Writing a Unified Paragraph

A good paragraph is **unified**. That means that all of the supporting sentences relate to the controlling idea in the topic sentence. They all belong in the paragraph.

Look again at the model paragraph. The topic sentence is *My cell phone camera has several advantages*. All of the supporting sentences describe the advantages of the camera, so the paragraph is unified.

When a sentence does not support the controlling idea, that sentence is **irrelevant**.

EXAMPLES

- I think most cell phones come with cameras today.
- I have another camera, too.

These sentences are irrelevant because they do not support the controlling idea in the topic sentence of the model paragraph. They do not describe advantages of the writer's cell phone camera.

Practice

Find the irrelevant sentence in each paragraph and cross it out.

1.   Computer viruses can cause a lot of trouble. Some viruses make computers run slowly. Some viruses make programs stop working. Some destroy files. ~~That happened to my brother.~~ Viruses can cost people a lot of time and money.

2. Spam is a big problem for me. It takes me a lot of time to delete these unwanted messages, and sometimes I delete messages from friends by mistake. I usually send them instant messages instead of e-mail. Sometimes my mailbox is full of spam, so it has no room for the mail I want. I really hate spam.

3. E-mail has many advantages over other kinds of communication. You can send messages faster than regular mail. You can easily send the same message to many people at the same time. Compared to the telephone, e-mail costs less, and you don't have to answer your mail right away. All e-mail users should have a virus protection program.

4. There are two important disadvantages to riding in elevators. First, when you ride in an elevator, you just stand there and don't get any exercise. People today don't get enough exercise, so they should avoid elevators and take the stairs. Some disabled people have to depend on elevators. Second, elevators can get stuck if there is a power failure, and being trapped in an elevator is a terrible experience. I recommend not using elevators.

WRITING SKILL

Using Commas

Commas have many uses. Here are three rules to remember.

1. Use a comma before *and*, *but*, *or*, or *so* in a compound sentence.

   EXAMPLES
   - I have a cell phone camera, **and** I use it a lot.
   - My cell phone camera doesn't take great photos, **but** they're good enough.
   - I can save the photos, **or** I can delete them.
   - My cell phone battery is low, **so** I need to charge it.

2. Use commas after items in a series of three or more.

   EXAMPLES
   - My cell phone is small, black, and shiny.
   - I use the camera to take pictures of my friends, my family, and my cat.

3. Use a comma after a word or phrase that introduces a sentence.

EXAMPLES

- **At home,** I transfer the photos from my cell phone to my computer.
- **Last month,** I got a new cell phone.
- **In addition,** it is easy to share photos.

Practice

A. **Look for commas in the model paragraph on page 98. Find an example of each comma rule and copy the sentence.**

1. commas in a series

   _____

2. a comma in a compound sentence

   _____

3. a comma after an introductory phrase

   _____

B. **Add commas to the sentences that need them. Three sentences do not need commas.**

1. Phishing e-mails look real, but they are not.
2. E-mail users have to deal with spam viruses and phishing e-mails.
3. Many people use e-mail both at work and at home.
4. At work I receive about 30 e-mails a day.
5. I often receive spam and I usually just delete it without reading it.
6. Spam often has ads for ways to make money look younger or lose weight.
7. Computer programs help block spam and kill viruses.
8. People may worry about viruses but they usually continue to use e-mail and visit websites.

C. **Write sentences with commas. Follow the directions.**

1. Write a compound sentence with *and, but, or,* or *so.*

   _____

2. Write a sentence with a series of three items.

   _____

3. Write two sentences. Begin each sentence with one of these introductory words or phrases: *Finally, Last week, On weekends,* or *For example*. Be sure to use two different words or phrases.

_____

_____

Editing

Read the paragraph. Correct the incomplete sentences, and fix the mistakes in punctuation and use of pronouns. There are eight mistakes including the example.

The Disadvantages of My Brother's Motorcycle

My brother has a motorcycle and there are several disadvantages to it. It is useful only in nice weather. A motorcycle rider can't see very well in the rain. He gets wet, too. In addition a motorcycle can carry only one or two people. It can carry some small things but it not good for grocery shopping for a family, for example. Most of all, a motorcycle is not safe. Nothing protects the rider in an accident so I worry about my brother. I want him to sell his motorcycle. Because of these disadvantages.

WRITING ASSIGNMENT

Write a paragraph. Follow the steps.

STEP 1   Get ideas.

A. Work in pairs. Add at least two more kinds of technology to the list.

cameras	cell phones	electric guitars	text messaging
cars	dishwashers	electronic dictionaries	videocameras

B. Choose two or three kinds of technology to talk about with your partner. Ask and answer the questions about each one.

1. How do you use it?
2. How is it helpful?
3. What problems does it have?

STEP 2   Organize your ideas.

A. Choose one kind of technology from Step 1. Make notes about it. Organize your notes like this.

Your Topic: _____	
Advantages	**Disadvantages**

B. Write about advantages or disadvantages of this technology as your topic. On a piece of paper, make an outline.

STEP 3   Write your paragraph.

Write your paragraph. Follow the outline you made in Step 2.

STEP 4   Check your work.

Read your paragraph. Use the writing checklist to look for mistakes, and use the editing checklist on page 192 to mark corrections.

Writing Checklist

❑ Did you use correct paragraph format?

❑ Did you describe advantages or disadvantages, not both?

❑ Did you place commas where you need them?

❑ Are subject and object pronouns used correctly?

❑ Is your paragraph unified, with no irrelevant sentences?

STEP 5   Write a final copy.

Correct your mistakes. Copy your final copy and give it to your instructor.

Using YouTube

In this chapter you will:

- read about sharing videos over the Internet

- learn about organizing by order of importance

- learn how to use connectors

- write a paragraph using connectors and the order of importance

PRE-READING

Discussion

Discuss the questions in pairs or small groups.

1. Look at the photo. What are the people doing and why?
2. Check (✔) the kinds of videos you enjoy watching or making.

   ____ videos of family   ____ music videos   ____ travel videos

   ____ funny videos   ____ other: _____
3. What are some reasons that people make videos?

Vocabulary

Read the boldfaced words and their definitions. Then complete each sentence with the correct word or phrase.

afterward:	after an event or time
complain:	say that you are annoyed or unhappy about something
entertain:	do something that interests people or makes them laugh
invite:	ask someone to come to a party, dinner, wedding, etc.
last:	continue to happen for a period of time
lonely:	unhappy because you are alone
look forward to:	be excited and happy about something that is going to happen
process:	a series of actions someone does to get a certain result

1. My friends and I made a video. _____*Afterward*_____, we showed it to our friends.

2. Making a movie is usually a difficult _____. It takes a lot of people and a lot of time.

3. When my phone line does not work, I call the phone company and _____.

4. Most movies _____ about two hours, but *Titanic* is three hours and 14 minutes long.

5. Many videos on the Internet _____ people. They are fun to watch.

6. I often _____ my friends to come to my house and watch a movie.

7. Many people like to watch videos online. They _____ seeing new ones.

8. We need friends to talk to. When we cannot talk to anyone, we often feel _____.

Using YouTube

1   In 2004, three young men went to a dinner party in San Francisco. **Afterward**, they wanted to share a video from the party with their friends. They wanted to send it over the Internet. But at the time, the **process** of sharing videos that way was difficult. Using e-mail did not work, and the friends **complained** that there was no website to help them. So they created their own. They called their website YouTube. It made sharing videos easy, so the website soon became very popular. People watched 2.5 billion videos in the first six months!

2   Today, more than 70,000 new videos go up on YouTube each day. People watch more than 1 billion videos a day. Many **last** no more than 10 minutes. These videos show all kinds of things, from sleeping cats to tornados.[1] Most of the filmmakers are not professionals. They are just everyday people making videos, and they use the website in a variety of interesting ways.

3   First, many people use YouTube to **entertain** others. One example is Judson Laipply. He made a funny dance video and put it on YouTube in 2006. People watched the video more than 10 million times in the first two weeks. Now people stop Judson on the street to ask, "Are you the dance guy on YouTube?" Some people have **invited** him to dance at their weddings. A few women have even asked to marry him. Judson wants to make more dance videos, and people **look forward to** seeing them.

4   Other people use YouTube to advertise a business. David Taub does this. He is a guitar teacher, and he sells videos of guitar lessons on his own website. He wanted to increase his business, so he put short videos with free lessons on YouTube. People enjoyed watching the lessons on YouTube, and afterward, many decided to go to David's own website. Soon David had a lot of new customers, and now he sells hundreds of guitar lesson videos each week.

5   People also use YouTube because they want to become famous. For example, many singers and music groups put videos on the website. They hope that music companies will see them and get in touch.[2] The group OK Go did that. They put an entertaining music video on YouTube that showed the group dancing on treadmills.[3] The video became popular very quickly. Later, the group was invited to sing and dance on MTV.

6   In addition, some people use YouTube to help others. Ryan Fitzgerald is one example. Ryan is a friendly young man who knows that some people are **lonely** and have no one to talk to. One day, he made a video of himself for YouTube. In the video, he gave his cell phone number and invited people to call him. In less than a week, he had more than 5,000 calls and messages from all over the world. These days, he is very busy talking on the phone. He helps people when he can, but mostly, he just listens, like a friend.

(continued)

---

[1]**tornado:** an extremely violent storm with winds that spin around very quickly

[2]**get in touch:** write or call someone
[3]**treadmill:** a piece of exercise equipment with a moving belt that you walk or run on while staying in place

7   Finally, some filmmakers use YouTube in a more serious way. They want to inform people about important events happening in the world. For example, they show clips[4] of videos from countries at war, or they show people in need of help after a storm. Sometimes TV news shows do not give enough information about these events. Thanks to YouTube filmmakers, people can go to their computers and learn more.

8   For many people, YouTube is more than just another website to visit. It is a way to communicate with others—to entertain them, help them, or inform them. More and more people are using it every day, and they will probably find even more ways to use it.

----

[4]**clip:** a short piece of a movie, video, or TV show

Identifying Main Ideas

Read each question. Circle the letter of the best answer.

1. What is the main idea of the reading?
   a. Many people use YouTube to become famous.
   b. People use the YouTube website in several interesting ways.
   c. YouTube is a website with millions of videos.

2. What is the main idea of paragraph 7?
   a. People use YouTube to tell others about world events.
   b. TV news shows do not inform people about world events.
   c. People can use YouTube to show war in other countries.

3. Which reason for using YouTube is NOT in the reading?
   a. People use YouTube to entertain others.
   b. People use YouTube to connect with other people.
   c. People use YouTube to show friends their vacation videos.

Identifying Details

Look at the reading again. Scan for numbers and complete the sentences.

1. In the first six months of YouTube, people watched more than _____2.5 billion_____ videos.

2. More than _____ videos a day go up on the YouTube website.

3. Every day, people watch more than _____ videos on YouTube.

4. Many videos on YouTube last no more than _____ minutes.

5. People watched Judson Laipply's video more than
_____ times in the first two weeks.

6. Ryan Fitzgerald had more than _____ calls and
messages in less than a week.

FROM READING TO WRITING

Reflecting on the Reading

Discuss the questions in pairs or small groups.

1. Some people use YouTube to learn about world events. How do you
learn about world events: the newspaper, TV, or the Internet? Which
gives you the best information?
2. Ryan Fitzgerald made a video and gave his cell phone number. Is this
a good way to connect with other people? Explain.
3. Have you visited the YouTube website? If so, describe your visit. If
not, do you plan to visit YouTube? Explain.

Activating Your Vocabulary

**Complete the sentences with the words from the box. Use capitals where
necessary.**

afterward	entertain	last	look forward to
complained	invited	lonely	~~process~~

1. It is not easy for me to make my own videos. It is a difficult
_____*process*_____ because there are so many steps.

2. Ryan Fitzgerald gave out his phone number and _____
people to call him.

3. My friends _____ about the poor quality of a video
they saw on YouTube.

4. I like funny animal videos. They really _____ me.

5. People who are _____ need someone to talk to.

6. Some YouTube videos are short and _____ only a few
minutes.

7. I have fun watching videos on YouTube, and I _____
my next visit to the website.

8. Ryan Fitzgerald gave his phone number on YouTube.
_____, thousands of people called him.

Read the model paragraph.

MODEL

> ### The Uses of a TV
>
> There are several ways to use a TV. First, you can use it to play video games. If you have a video game console, like a Nintendo or PlayStation, you can connect it to your TV. A big TV screen is great for viewing video games. Second, you can use a TV with a VCR or a DVD player. You can buy or rent your favorite movies and watch them when you want. Most of all, you can use a TV to watch TV programs such as daily news and weather, current sitcoms and dramas, or sports from around the world. You can watch programs like these on channels in other languages, too. You can use a TV in all of these ways either alone or with friends. In conclusion, a TV is a very useful kind of technology.

WRITING SKILL

Organizing by Order of Importance

When you write a paragraph with a list of advantages, disadvantages, reasons, or other ideas, plan the order of your paragraph carefully. Put the least important idea first and the most important one last so that you end the paragraph with your strongest point.

Practice

A. Look again at the model paragraph. Which use of a TV does the writer think is least important? Which use is most important?

1. Least important: _____

2. Most important: _____

B. Decide on the order of importance for these sentences. Write 1 for least important, 2 for more important, and 3 for most important.

_____ 1. E-mail messages carrying viruses can cause very serious problems with your computer, so get a virus protection program.

_____ 2. There is a lot of spam on the Internet, so you may get unwanted messages.

_____ 3. Phishing e-mails can fool people, so be careful about giving personal information.

C. Complete the paragraph. Copy the sentences from Exercise B in order from least to most important.

E-mail is very useful, but it can bring you problems, too. First of all,

_____

In addition, _____

Most important, _____

_____

E-mail is great if you use it with care.

Using Connectors

WRITING SKILL

Connectors are words that show relationships between ideas and sentences. They often introduce a new idea or show the organization of information in a paragraph. Look at the list of connectors below.

first	finally	moreover
second	first of all	most of all
third	in addition	in conclusion

Put a comma after a connector that introduces a sentence.

EXAMPLE

• **Most of all,** a TV helps people get information they need.

Practice

A. Look again at the model paragraph. Circle the connectors. How many are there? _____

B. Complete the paragraph with connectors. Use commas when necessary.

There are four main reasons for the success of YouTube. (1) _____ YouTube made it easy to put videos online. That means friends can now share videos quickly and even show them to the whole world. (2) _____ the creators of YouTube set up one central place to find video clips of all kinds. People can go to this one website for videos on every possible topic. (3) _____ it is not hard to find the videos you want at YouTube. You can find them in more than one way. (4) _____ YouTube gives people a place to put TV clips so they can share and enjoy their favorite shows.

Editing

Read the paragraph. Correct the incomplete sentences, and fix the mistakes in punctuation and use of connectors. There are six mistakes including the example.

Using the Internet

I use the Internet in several ways. First⌃I use the Internet to get sports information. Because I want to read about my favorite teams back home. Third, I use the Internet for e-mail and instant messages. For example I get e-mail from my college, and I get instant messages from my brothers and my friends. In addition I use the Internet to go to Facebook. I can read about my friends, write to them, look at photos, or find new friends. Finally I use the Internet for music. I go online every day to watch music videos and download songs. I have thousands of songs on my computer. I cannot imagine life without the Internet.

WRITING ASSIGNMENT

Write a paragraph. Follow the steps.

STEP 1 **Get ideas.**

A. Choose a topic for your paragraph. For kinds of technology, look back at the list on page 101 in Chapter 9. (Do not choose the same technology you wrote about in Chapter 9.)

❑ **Topic 1:** Advantages of one kind of technology

❑ **Topic 2:** Advantages of using the Internet

B. On a piece of paper, make a chart like this one about your topic. Think of at least three advantages or uses.

ADVANTAGES OF USING THE INTERNET	
Use	**Examples**
get the news	world news, sports, weather

C. Work in pairs. Ask and answer the questions about your topic.

1. Which use is most important?
2. Which one is least important?

STEP 2   **Organize your ideas.**

A. Write a topic sentence for your paragraph.

_____

B. On a piece of paper, make an outline. Choose ideas that support your paragraph from the chart you made for Step 1. Write the sentences in order of importance, with the most important idea last. Use connectors to introduce the sentences.

STEP 3   **Write your paragraph.**

Write your paragraph. Follow the outline you made in Step 2.

STEP 4   **Check your work.**

Read your paragraph. Use the Writing Checklist to look for mistakes, and use the editing symbols on page 192 to mark corrections.

Writing Checklist

❑ Did you use correct paragraph format?
❑ Did you organize your ideas by order of importance?
❑ Did you use connectors to introduce new ideas?
❑ Did you place commas where you need them?
❑ Is your paragraph unified, with no irrelevant sentences?

STEP 5   **Write a final copy.**

Correct your mistakes. Copy your final paragraph and give it to your instructor.

In Business and at Work

In this chapter you will:

- read an article about a successful business

- learn about skimming a reading

- write a paragraph with examples

The Success of Starbucks

Discussion

Discuss the questions in pairs or small groups.

1. Look at the photo. What type of business do you see? What do people do there?
2. How often do people drink coffee in your country? Where do they drink it?
3. The Starbucks company has cafés around the world. Why do you think Starbucks cafés are popular?

Vocabulary

Read the boldfaced words and their definitions. Then complete each paragraph with the correct words or phrases.

attract:	make someone like or feel interested in something
characteristics:	qualities that something or someone usually has
expert:	someone with special skills or knowledge of a subject
improve:	make something better
original:	new and different
quality:	how good something is
tradition:	something that people have done for a long time and continue to do
turn out:	happen in a particular way or have a particular result

The new owners of the restaurant La Tavola Romana were not happy with the (1) _____quality_____ of the food. So they looked for a new chef to make the food better. They offered a high salary to (2) _____ people with a lot of experience. They hired a new chef who promises to (3) _____ the food. He will follow a longtime Italian (4) _____ for many dishes, but he also has some (5) _____ ideas for new dishes.

Gianni Vitale, the author of *In the Italian Kitchen*, is a well-known (6) _____ on Italian cooking. He says that (7) _____ of good Italian cooking include the use of fresh ingredients. He says, "You must begin with fresh ingredients if you want a dish to (8) _____ well."

Skimming

Skimming is reading something very quickly in order to find the main ideas. To skim a paragraph, first read the first two sentences and the concluding sentence, while glancing at the details.

Skimming is helpful when you have a lot to read and you want to understand the most important information. When you skim, do not read every word or look up words in a dictionary. To skim a reading, follow these steps:

1. Read the title.
2. Read the first paragraph. It usually gives an introduction to the reading and states the main idea.
3. Read the first sentence of each paragraph that follows. The first sentence often tells you the topic and main idea of the paragraph.
4. Read the last paragraph, or the conclusion. It often repeats the main idea.

Practice

A. Skim the paragraph. What is the main idea?

_____

Many people would like to have their own café, but what is the secret to its success? Expert Alex Finkel says the most important factors are the right location, an attractive design, speed and efficiency, marketing, and taste. The best locations are near colleges or on busy walking streets. In addition to location, the café must be attractive and serve coffee quickly. Good marketing means a menu that appeals to customers. Finally, good-tasting coffee is very important. Following these rules will increase your chances of having a successful coffee bar business.

B. Look at the list of topics for the first five paragraphs in "The Success of Starbucks" on pages 117–118. Then skim the reading and identify the topic of each paragraph. Write the paragraph number next to its topic.

_¶4_ 1. keeping customers happy

_____ 2. the beginning of Starbucks

_____ 3. creating an original business

_____ 4. making a good product

_____ 5. keeping employees happy

C. Compare answers with your classmates'. Then read the whole article.

The Success of Starbucks

1   "I'd like to start my own business." Is this something you ever say to yourself? Many people share this dream. Howard Schultz was thinking about starting a business of his own when he traveled to Italy on vacation back in 1982. While he was there, he stopped at a café and had a cup of coffee. He liked the coffee, but more importantly, he liked the comfortable atmosphere[1] of the café. It made him think, "Maybe I can go into the café business back home." When he returned to the United States, he opened a café and called it *Il Giornale*. He later renamed it Starbucks. It **turned out** that people liked the café so much that, over time, his business grew from one café to thousands all over the world. Starbucks has been successful because it has four important **characteristics**.

2   First, Starbucks succeeded because Howard Schultz had an **original** idea. In 1982, most Americans weren't familiar with the European **tradition** of drinking gourmet[2] coffee in nice cafés. Most Americans drank only instant coffee,[3] and they usually drank it at home. Howard Schultz thought that Americans would like the European way. When he opened his café, it was a hit with customers partly because it was new and different. Customers came back again and again, and they brought their friends. They stayed to talk and bought more coffee. The café **attracted** a lot of customers because it was a new kind of business.

3   A good product is also important to a company's success, and Starbucks is very serious about its coffee. The company has **experts** who know a lot about coffee and travel to various countries to find it. They choose only the best-**quality** coffee beans. They take the beans back to the United States and make coffee from them. After they taste the coffee, they decide whether or not to buy more of those beans. The experts also help farmers **improve** the quality of the beans they grow. Starbucks does a lot to make sure that it offers a good product.

4   From the start, Schultz has believed in keeping customers happy. He feels that they should be able to stay as long as they want, and they should get fast service. Schultz also believes that customers should get exactly what they want, so at Starbucks, customers can get their coffee made their own special way. Also, some people do not want to stay and drink their coffee, so Starbucks has drive-throughs[4] to give them faster service. Starbucks does all these things to keep customers happy.

5   Schultz also believes that a company should take care of its employees, so Starbucks is good to its employees in several ways. For example, Starbucks gives the same benefits[5] to part-time employees that it gives to full-time employees. Starbucks also pays its

(continued)

---

[1]**atmosphere:** the feeling that a place or situation gives you

[2]**instant coffee:** coffee prepared quickly by adding hot water to coffee in powder form from a jar

[3]**gourmet:** relating to very good quality food or drink

[4]**drive-through:** a service you can use without getting out of your car

[5]**benefits:** vacation time, medical insurance, or other good things you get from a job

employees a little more money than other companies do. In addition, company leaders often call stores to say thank you to the employees, and they ask employees for suggestions on ways to improve. In all these ways, Starbucks makes its employees feel respected and valued. In January 2007, the popular business magazine *Fortune* voted Starbucks one of the best companies to work for in the United States.

6   Starbucks has the characteristics that many businesses need to succeed. If you think you'd like to start your own business, then keep Howard Schultz's story in mind. You may want to follow his lead.

Identifying Main Ideas

Match the business characteristics in the box with the details from the reading. Write the characteristic on the correct line.

~~keeping customers happy~~	providing a good product
making your business original	keeping employees happy

1. _keeping customers happy_
   a. The service is fast.
   b. Customers get what they want.
   c. Customers stay as long as they want.

2. _____
   a. Experts travel the world to look for the best coffee beans.
   b. They help farmers improve their coffee beans.
   c. Experts taste all the coffee.

3. _____
   a. Employees get good benefits.
   b. Starbucks pays employees more.
   c. Company leaders call stores to say thank you to employees.

4. _____
   a. Schultz's first café introduced a European tradition.
   b. It was a new kind of restaurant for Americans.
   c. The coffee was different from the usual American coffee.

Identifying Details

A. Complete each sentence. Circle the letter of the best answer.

1. Howard Schultz traveled to _____.
   a. France   b. Italy   c. Germany

2. Thirty years ago, many Americans drank only _____ coffee.
   a. gourmet   b. instant   c. strong

3. Schultz's first café was called _____.
   a. Starbucks   b. Coffee Café   c. *Il Giornale*

4. In January 2007, _____ magazine voted Starbucks one of the best companies to work for in the United States
   a. *Time*   b. *Newsweek*   c. *Fortune*

B. Mark the statements T (true) or F (false). Correct the false statements.

_____ 1. Howard Schultz traveled to Italy in 1982 and got the idea for a café.

_____ 2. Starbucks grows its own coffee beans.

_____ 3. Starbucks has employees who travel to foreign countries to buy its coffee beans.

_____ 4. Part-time employees at Starbucks do not receive benefits.

_____ 5. The Starbucks drive-through gives people coffee to go, but it has slow service.

_____ 6. Employees at Starbucks feel like the company respects them.

FROM READING TO WRITING

Reflecting on the Reading

Discuss the questions in pairs or small groups.

1. Which of the following characteristics of a good business is the most important one? Why?
   - making your business original
   - providing a good product
   - keeping customers happy
   - keeping employees happy

2. Do you know a business that has one of the four characteristics? Explain how the business has this characteristic.

Activating Your Vocabulary

A. *Complete the sentences with the words from the box.*

attract	experts	~~original~~	tradition
characteristics	improve	quality	turn out

1. Today, people are used to seeing European-style cafés in the United States, but in 1982, it was an _____*original*_____ idea.

2. Some businesses advertise on the Internet to _____ customers.

3. Companies sometimes say to customers, "We want to offer you better service. How can we _____ it?"

4. Some people don't care much about the _____ of the coffee they drink. It doesn't really matter to them if the coffee is good or bad; they just want it hot and strong.

5. Successful businesses often share certain _____.

6. The managers of some companies ask the employees for ideas to improve customer service. They think the employees can be _____ on what customers want.

7. Sometimes a business idea sounds great, but when it is put into practice, it doesn't _____ well.

8. Every summer, the company has a picnic for its employees. This _____ is one way that the company says thank you.

B. *Complete the paragraph with four words from Exercise A.*

A few cafés in the world are very (**1**) _____. They are special because they are café/laundromats. These cafés, in Copenhagen, San Francisco, and New York, share some (**2**) _____. They are places where people can do their laundry and drink coffee. They also (**3**) _____ customers with other services like music entertainment. Perhaps these cafés will become a new popular (**4**) _____ in cities.

Read the model paragraph.

MODEL

My Dream Business

My computer-training center will have several important characteristics. First, my center will provide good customer service. For example, students will be able to take classes or get individual help. The classes will be at different times for people with a variety of schedules, and I will also have classes in different languages. In addition, the center will have a friendly atmosphere. For instance, I will serve free coffee and snacks. The center will be a comfortable place for people to meet. Lastly, I will provide quality teaching. For example, I will find good teachers who know a lot about computers. The teachers will also be very patient. These characteristics will make my business successful.

WRITING SKILL

Using Examples as Supporting Details

In Chapter 5, you practiced writing sentences that give examples. Example sentences often begin with *For example* or *For instance* followed by a comma and a complete sentence.

EXAMPLE

- The store has convenient hours. **For example**, on weekdays it opens at 9:00 A.M. and stays open until 9:00 P.M.

Good writers use examples to support their ideas. In the model paragraph above the writer uses examples to explain the characteristics of the business in more detail. Study this outline of the paragraph:

Topic sentence:	My computer-training center will have several important characteristics.
Characteristic 1:	First, my center will provide good customer service.
Example:	For example, students will be able to take classes or get individual help.
Characteristic 2:	In addition, the center will have a friendly atmosphere.
Example:	For instance, I will serve free coffee and snacks.
Characteristic 3:	Lastly, I will provide quality teaching.
Example:	I will find good teachers who know a lot about computers.

Practice

A. Use ideas from the reading on pages 117–118 to complete the outline.

Topic sentence: Starbucks has been successful because it has four important characteristics.

Characteristic 1: The concept was original.

Example: *It serves European-style coffee.*

Characteristic 2: Starbucks makes sure its product is good.

Example: _____

Characteristic 3: Starbucks keeps its customers happy.

Example: _____

Characteristic 4: Starbucks keeps its employees happy.

Example: _____

B. Read the paragraph. Circle the three characteristics. Underline the examples.

Aiea Bowl in Hawaii is a unique business for several reasons. First, it has an exciting bowling alley. For example, it was voted Hawaii's best bowling alley in 2009. Second, the bowling alley has an amazing restaurant with a big menu. For example, you can get mahi-mahi, pork, or a mushroom burger. Last, Aiea Bowl is a great place to meet up with friends. For instance, Aiea Bowl has DJs playing music, dancing, and a lounge. I love going to Aiea Bowl.

C. Read the sentences. Write an example for each one.

1. My uncle has a customer-friendly flower shop.

   For example, he always gets his customers the flowers they want.

2. The owner of Anne's Clothing wants her employees to be happy.

   _____

3. Customers get fast service at Taylor's Dry Cleaning.

   _____

4. The atmosphere at Magic Nail Salon is very relaxing.

   _____

5. The menu at my favorite restaurant is very original.

   _____

Editing

Read the paragraph. Correct the incomplete sentences, and fix the mistakes in capitalization, punctuation, and verb tense. There are eight mistakes including the example.

Sugar Bowl Bakery

Sugar Bowl Bakery is a successful business for several reasons. First of all, the owners ^*are* hard workers. When the Ly brothers come from Vietnam in 1979, they don't have much money, but they were ready to work. In 1984, they open a bakery in San Francisco and worked long hours. Now they have several stores. Second, the Ly brothers went out and looked for customers. For example, they took their cakes and cookies to hospitals, hotels, restaurants, and supermarkets around the city. they found new customers instead of waiting for the customers to find them. Third they have original product. Their bakers try new recipes all the time. For instance, their blueberry chip cookies. Finally, the brothers care about their employees. Andrew Ly says, "Our employees are like family members." As a result, the employees feel special. My cousin is proud to work in one of the bakeries. Today, the success of the Ly brothers encourages other new business owners.

WRITING ASSIGNMENT

Write a paragraph. Follow the steps.

STEP 1 **Get ideas.**

A. Choose a topic for your paragraph. Work in pairs.

❏ **Topic 1:** Characteristics of a successful business you know

Think of three successful businesses. Make a chart listing their names. Under each name, list the characteristics of that business.

❑ **Topic 2:** Characteristics of a business you want to start

Think about the kind of business you want to start, where it would be, and who would use it. Make a chart with three columns for: 1) Kind of business 2) Its location 3) Who the customers are

B. Work in pairs. Discuss your notes.

C. Write a paragraph about the topic you chose. List at least three positive characteristics of the business.

Topic: _____

Characteristic 1: _____

Characteristic 2: _____

Characteristic 3: _____

STEP 2   **Organize your ideas.**

A. Write a topic sentence for your paragraph.

_____

EXAMPLES

- My favorite restaurant has three important characteristics.
- My accounting business will be successful for several reasons.

B. On a piece of paper, make an outline like the one below. Choose characteristics from Step 1 to support the topic sentence. Give an example to support each characteristic.

Topic sentence:

Characteristic 1:

Supporting detail:

Characteristic 2:

Supporting detail:

Characteristic 3:

Supporting detail:

Concluding sentence:

STEP 3   **Write your paragraph.**

Write your paragraph. Follow the outline you made in Step 2.

STEP 4   **Check your work.**

Read your paragraph. Use the writing checklist to look for mistakes, and use the editing symbols on page 192 to mark corrections.

Writing Checklist

❑ Does your paragraph have a topic sentence and a concluding sentence?

❑ Have you included at least three characteristics of the business?

❑ Did you include examples to support the characteristics?

❑ Did you write complete sentences, with subjects and verbs?

❑ Did you use correct punctuation?

STEP 5   **Write a final copy.**

Correct your mistakes. Copy your final paragraph and give it to your instructor.

**In this chapter
you will:**

• read about
happiness at
work

• learn how to
avoid sentence
fragments and
run-on sentences

• write a
descriptive
paragraph

Happiness at Work

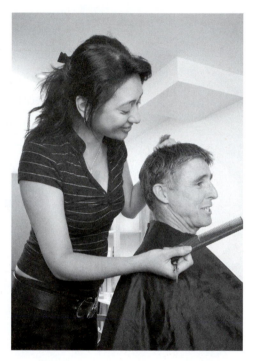

PRE-READING

Discussion

Discuss the questions in pairs or small groups.

1. Look at the photos. What jobs are the people doing?
2. Do the jobs look interesting to you? Why or why not?
3. What careers do you think would make you happy?

Vocabulary

Read the sentences. Match the boldfaced words with the definitions in the box.

_h_ 1. I don't know how much Pam earns at her job, but I **estimate** that she makes about $50,000 a year.

____ 2. Matt likes his job. He's **satisfied** with it. He doesn't want to change jobs.

____ 3. Lisa changed jobs **recently**, and she likes her new job a lot.

____ 4. A career counselor helps people **figure out** what kind of work they want to do.

____ 5. Alma wants to learn about careers in nursing, so she's going to do **research** in that field of work in the library.

____ 6. The president of the company will visit today so some employees will **get to** meet him.

____ 7. Some jobs are bad for people's **health**, so workers in those jobs often get sick or hurt.

____ 8. The employee **responses** to the new health insurance plan were mostly positive.

---

a. be able to do something and feel lucky to have that opportunity

b. study a subject to discover new facts about it

c. what you say or write as an answer to something

d. the condition of your body and your mind

e. find an answer to a problem

f. pleased because something is good or because you have achieved something

g. not long ago

h. make a reasonable guess at the size, amount, or time of something

---

Happiness at Work

1   "Find a job you love, and you'll never work a day in your life." Do you agree with this old saying?[1] Joanne Gordon does. She is the author of *Be Happy at Work* and other books about careers. Gordon **estimates** that about 30 percent of employees in North America do not like their jobs, and she thinks that is terrible. She wants to help people who do not feel **satisfied** with their jobs find work that is good for them. Now, some may say that only a few kinds of jobs can really make someone happy, but the truth is that many different kinds of work can be enjoyable and rewarding. Joanne says, "There are no happy jobs, only happy workers." She believes that happy workers share three main characteristics.

2   First, happy workers enjoy the daily activities of their jobs, and they look forward to the workday. Take Tony Hawk, for example. At age 14, he became a professional skateboarder; at 16, he was the best in the world. Now he is a businessman working on projects related to skateboarding—films and video games, for example—but he still skates every day. He once said, "My youngest son's pre-school class was **recently** asked what their dads do for work. The **responses** were things like 'My dad sells money' and 'My dad **figures** stuff[2] **out**.' My son said, 'I've never seen my dad do work.'" Tony agrees that his job doesn't look like work, and it doesn't feel like work, either. He has found a way to spend each day doing a job he enjoys.

3   Second, happy workers like the people they work with. Sally Ayote says, "I work with the coolest[3] people in the world." She and her crew[4] cook for almost 1,200 people in Antarctica. Most of these people are scientists who are doing **research**. Sally loves to sit and talk with them. She says, "There is no television here, no radio, so I **get to** know the scientists and what they're studying." Sally thinks she has a great job, and the best part about it is the people.

4   Third, happy workers know that their work helps others. Caroline Baron's work helps refugees, people who have had to leave their home countries because of war or other dangers. She is a filmmaker who started an organization called FilmAid, which shows movies in refugee camps around the world. Caroline believes that movies can be very helpful in these camps. For one thing, entertaining movies let refugees forget their troubles for a little while. Movies can also teach important subjects like **health** and safety. For example, in one camp, thousands of refugees saw a movie about how to get clean water. Caroline knows that many refugees are glad to have the film program.[5] One refugee said, "FilmAid makes people happy. It makes people come together in peace." Caroline knows that she is helping other people, and this makes her feel proud and happy about her work.

[3]**cool:** slang (informal) used to show that you like or admire someone or something
[4]**crew:** a group of people who work together doing a specific job
[5]**program:** a set of organized activities that people do to achieve something

[1]**saying:** a phrase that most people know that gives advice about life
[2]**stuff:** (informal) a number of different things, activities, or subjects

5   Tony Hawk, Sally Ayote, and Caroline Baron all get great satisfaction from their work. But is happiness at work really important? Tony Hawk believes it is. He says, "Find the thing you love. If you are doing what you love, there is much more happiness there than being rich or famous." Joanne Gordon would agree. She encourages people to find something they enjoy doing, find people they like to work with, and find ways to help others. Then they can be proud of what they do, and they will probably be happy at work.

Gordon, Joanne. *Be Happy At Work* (excerpt). New York: Random House, 2005.

Identifying Main Ideas

Read each question. Circle the letter of the best answer.

1. What is the main idea of the reading?
   a. People who are happy at their jobs have three main characteristics.
   b. Most people in the United States do not feel happy in their careers.
   c. It is important for people to enjoy the daily activities of their jobs.

2. What is the main idea of paragraph 3?
   a. It is important to like the people with whom you work.
   b. Sally Ayote works with the coolest people in the world.
   c. Working with scientists is fun and interesting.

3. What is the main idea of paragraph 4?
   a. Movies encourage people to forget the difficult times in their lives.
   b. Films can help teach refugees about important subjects.
   c. Caroline Baron is happy because she knows her work helps others.

Identifying Details

Look at the reading again. Match the statements with the people who made them. (Note: There is one extra person.)

STATEMENTS		PEOPLE
_f_	1. "There are no happy jobs, only happy workers."	a. Tony Hawk
____	2. "I've never seen my dad do work."	b. Tony Hawk's son
____	3. "I work with the coolest people in the world."	c. Caroline Baron
____	4. "FilmAid makes people happy."	d. a refugee
____	5. "Find the thing you love."	e. Sally Ayote
		f. Joanne Gordon

Reflecting on the Reading

Discuss the questions in pairs or small groups.

1. Do you have a job right now? If you do, how satisfied are you with your work?
2. The reading lists three characteristics of happy workers. Which characteristic is most important to you? Explain.
3. Is happiness at work really necessary? Can you be happy if you do not love your job? Explain.

Activating Your Vocabulary

Which sentence is closest in meaning to the one with the boldfaced word or phrase? Circle the letter.

1. You can do **research** on careers in the library.
   a. You can make decisions about careers.
   b. You can look for information about careers.

2. We **recently** read "Happiness at Work."
   a. We read it a little while ago.
   b. We read it carefully.

3. Sometimes people **get to** do a job that really makes them happy.
   a. Some people are lucky to have a job that makes them happy.
   b. Some people avoid a job that makes them happy.

4. The U.S. Bureau of Labor Statistics **estimates** that more than 3,000,000 Americans work in computer-related careers.
   a. They set a goal of 3,000,000.
   b. They guess that 3,000,000 is the right number.

5. Joanne Gordon says too many Americans are not **satisfied** with their jobs.
   a. They are not happy with them.
   b. They are not well-prepared for them.

6. The **responses** to the survey showed that most people would like more vacation time.
   a. Most people answered that they would like more vacation time.
   b. Most people declined to take more vacation time.

7. Before choosing a career, **figure out** what is most important to you.

    a. Discuss what is most important to you with other people.

    b. Think about and decide what is most important to you.

8. Is being happy in your work important for good **health**?

    a. Is it important for the state of your mind and body?

    b. Is it important for a good future?

WRITING

Read the model paragraph.

MODEL

A Good Job for Me

I am very satisfied with my job as a restaurant manager. First, I enjoy the daily activities of my job. I meet many interesting customers, and I enjoy solving problems at the restaurant. For example, sometimes many customers come all at one time. I like to figure out how to give them really fast service. Second, I know my work helps others. For instance, customers come to restaurants to relax and have a good time, and I like to make sure their meals are enjoyable. Lastly, I like the people I work with. As a manager, I get to know the staff very well. Sometimes they come to me for advice. I also have a very nice employer who is kind and pays me well. I think that my job is the right job for me.

WRITING
SKILL

Avoiding Sentence Fragments

A **sentence fragment** is a piece of a sentence. It looks like a sentence, but it is incomplete. Sometimes it is missing a subject or a verb (or both). Sometimes it is a dependent clause or a phrase that needs to be connected to a main clause. Look at the examples.

SENTENCE FRAGMENTS	PROBLEM
Enjoys his work.	The verb *enjoy* has no subject.
The people in my office.	The subject *people* has no verb.
Because I get satisfaction from helping others.	A dependent clause with *because* needs a main clause.
After I started my new job at Northeast United Bank.	A (dependent) time clause needs a main clause.

You can correct a sentence fragment by:

1. adding words

   ┌──── FRAGMENT ────┐
   - The people in my office.
   - The people in my office **are good team members**.

2. connecting the fragment to a complete sentence before or after it

   ┌──────── FRAGMENT ────────┐
   - Because I enjoy helping animals.
   - Because I enjoy helping animals, **I want to become a veterinarian.**
   - **I want to become a veterinarian** because I enjoy helping animals.

WRITING SKILL

Avoiding Run-on Sentences

A **run-on sentence** is not a correct sentence. A run-on sentence results when a writer does not connect two sentences correctly. Either the sentence is missing punctuation, or a comma is incorrectly placed. (This error is called a **comma splice**.) Look at the examples.

RUN-ON SENTENCES	PROBLEM
I want to be a nurse it's a good job for me.	Two complete sentences need correct punctuation (e.g. a period).
I will finish my education, then I will work.	*Then* cannot connect two main clauses.
I enjoy working at the café, it has a nice atmosphere.	A comma cannot connect sentences.
I expect to graduate next year, after I can begin my career.	*After* cannot directly follow a comma.

You can correct a run-on sentence by:

1. making two sentences
   - I want to be a nurse. **It's a good job for me.**
2. connecting sentences with *and, but, so,* or *or*
   - I will finish my education, **and** then I will work.
3. removing a comma splice
   - I expect to begin my career after I graduate next year.

Practice

A. Check (✔) the sentences that are complete. Write frag next to sentence fragments.

frag   1. A job in a place with a comfortable atmosphere.

_____ 2. I hope to find a high-paying job.

_____ 3. Because I need to support my family.

_____ 4. I think that teaching is a rewarding profession.

_____ 5. Serving customers with a smile and a friendly attitude.

_____ 6. He makes his employees feel respected and valued.

_____ 7. After I finish graduate school.

_____ 8. When I think about happiness at work.

B. Find the four fragments in the following paragraph and correct them. Then compare paragraphs with a partner.

it's a good choice

Engineering will be a good job for me for several reasons. First, ∧ because I am good at math and science. I am also good at working as part of a team, and engineers often work in teams. In addition, an important part of engineering is solving problems. Interesting work, in my opinion. Because I like challenges. Also, engineers can make a lot of money. To support my family. For all these reasons, I look forward to a career in engineering.

C. Work in pairs. Check (✔) the sentences that are correct. Write run-on next to the run-on sentences. Correct the run-on sentences.

so

run-on   1. I like working with children, ∧ I want to teach in a daycare center.

_____ 2. Because I am interested in land use and growing crops, I want a career in agriculture as an advisor to farmers.

_____ 3. I enjoy working in construction the pay is good.

(continued)

_____ 4. After I finish this program, I plan to apply to the nursing program.

_____ 5. I will get my degree in two years, then after, I will return to work in our family business.

_____ 6. I like my job at the Student Center, it is fun to meet other students.

_____ 7. Some day, I hope to be a college professor, I would like to teach economics and do research.

_____ 8. Before I can begin my career, I need to get more training.

Editing

Read the paragraph. Correct the incomplete sentences, and fix the mistakes in capitalization, punctuation, and subject-verb agreement. There are six mistakes including the example.

My Career Plans

I hope to become a businessman in the future⊙I would like to work for a large company with a good history. A job at a company like this bring me respect and other benefits. People will know the company and trust its products. They will respect me. Because I work for a company with a famous name. Like Toyota or Sony. I also might have the chance to travel. To other countries to represent the company. When I get this job, after, I will have a good salary and job security. I hope to have a long and successful career as a businessman.

WRITING ASSIGNMENT

Write a paragraph. Follow the steps.

STEP 1   **Get ideas.**

A. Choose a topic for your paragraph.

❑ **Topic 1:** A job you enjoy doing now

❑ **Topic 2:** A job you want to have some day

B. Decide on a job you want to write about. When people think about a job, they consider the following things. Check (✔) the ones that are most important to you.

_____ daily activities

_____ people you work with

_____ pay

_____ benefits

_____ schedule

_____ location

_____ goals of the job

_____ other: _____

C. Work in pairs. Ask and answer questions about the things you checked above.

STEP 2   **Organize your ideas.**

A. Complete a topic sentence for your paragraph.

Topic 1: I am satisfied with my job as a _____.

Topic 2: Some day, I want to work as a _____.

B. On a piece of paper, make an outline. Look back at your ideas in Step 1. Write supporting sentences for your topic sentence. Add a concluding sentence.

STEP 3   **Write your paragraph.**

Write your paragraph. Follow the outline you made in Step 2.

STEP 4 Check your work.

Read your paragraph. Use the Writing Checklist to look for mistakes, and use the editing symbols on page 192 to mark corrections.

> ### Writing Checklist
>
> ❑ Did you include a topic sentence?
>
> ❑ Did you write supporting sentences that relate to your topic sentence?
>
> ❑ Did you include characteristics of the job you are describing?
>
> ❑ Did you include examples to support the characteristics of the job?
>
> ❑ Did you check for sentence fragments and run-on sentences?

STEP 5 Write a final copy.

Correct your mistakes. Copy your final paragraph and give it to your instructor.

UNIT SEVEN

Music

A Gift of Music

*In this chapter
you will:*

• read a true story
about a strange
experience

• learn to make
inferences

• write a narrative
paragraph with
adverbs and
time clauses

Lionello Balestrieri's Frederick Chopin (1810–1849) Composing His Preludes

PRE-READING

Discussion

Discuss the questions in pairs or small groups.

1. Look at the picture. Who was Chopin? What was he famous for?
    When did he live?
2. Do you like music? If so, how old were you when you first became
    interested in music?
3. How important is music in your everyday life?
4. What things (such as art, music, books) have influenced (changed)
    your life? Explain.

Vocabulary

Read the sentences. Match the boldfaced words with the definitions in the box.

<u>g</u> **1.** The musician does not like to play any **compositions** but his own.

_____ **2.** That symphony is an **emotional** piece of music and always makes me cry.

_____ **3.** Lisa bowed as the **audience** clapped after her dance performance.

_____ **4.** The **flash** of the camera made the performers' eyes hurt.

_____ **5.** Many doctors **have trouble** telling bad news to the families of sick people.

_____ **6.** The **damage** to Juan's hand after the accident made it impossible for him to play the piano.

_____ **7.** My brother was upset when we went to the concert, but he felt better when the music gave him a feeling of **peace**.

_____ **8.** Molly often has very bad headaches. She has an unusual way of getting rid of her headaches: playing the piano. As soon as she starts playing, the headaches **go away**.

---

  a. find (doing something) difficult
  b. people watching or listening to a play, concert, speech, etc.
  c. a sudden quick bright light
  d. relating to one's feelings
  e. stop or disappear
  f. hurt or harm that breaks or destroys something
  g. music or poetry that someone writes
  h. quiet and calm

A Gift of Music

1   Tony Cicoria is a surgeon.[1] He is a very good doctor, and until 1994, his medical career and his family were the most important things in his life. But all of that changed at a payphone[2] in 1994. He was calling his mother at the time. As Tony explains, "The weather was pleasant, but I could see storm clouds in the distance. After the call, I was still holding the receiver[3] when I heard [a] . . . crack[4] and saw a **flash** of light come out of the phone and hit me in the face."

2   Tony remembers looking down at his own body on the floor. There were a lot of people around him, and a woman was performing CPR.[5] He thought that he was dead. Then he was surrounded by a bluish-white light. He remembers a deep feeling of **peace**. At the same time, he felt very excited about where he was going. But then suddenly, he was back inside his body. The bluish-white light and the peaceful feeling were gone, and his head and leg hurt, but other than that, he was fine. Believe it or not, he never even went to the hospital.

3   However, a few days later, Tony started to feel strange, so he went to see a neurologist.[6] Tony told him that he had been hit by lightning.[7] The neurologist did some tests, and everything looked fine. For the next week, Tony **had trouble** remembering people's names and the names of some illnesses, but those problems soon **went away**. It seemed that his near-death experience had not done any lasting **damage**.

4   But two weeks later, something much stranger started to happen to Tony. He suddenly became completely obsessed[8] with piano music. This was especially strange because Tony had never been interested in music before. He started listening to Chopin[9] all of the time. Then, one year after the lightning strike, he started to have dreams about music in which he was playing piano in a concert hall,[10] in front of a large **audience**. The music was not Chopin, however; he was playing one of his own musical **compositions**.

5   When he woke up from the dream, he wanted to write down the music. But there was one big problem: He could not read or write music. So Tony started taking piano lessons. Music became the most important thing in his life, and he heard it playing in his head all of the time, like a radio. He began to get up at 4:00 A.M. and play piano until 6:30 A.M., when he had to leave for work. When he got

---

[1]**surgeon:** a doctor who cuts open someone's body to fix or replace something inside
[2]**payphone:** a telephone you can use by putting coins or a card into it
[3]**receiver:** the part of a telephone that you hold next to your mouth and ear
[4]**crack:** a loud, short, sudden noise
[5]**perform CPR:** to do a set of actions (Cardio Pulmonary Resuscitation) to help someone who has stopped breathing or whose heart has stopped beating
[6]**neurologist:** a doctor who studies the nervous system and the diseases that are related to it

[7]**lightning:** a bright flash of light in the sky that happens during a storm
[8]**obsessed:** thinking only of one thing and unable to think about anything else
[9]**Chopin:** A pianist and piano composer of the Romantic period (19th century). Chopin is considered to be one of the greatest composers for the piano.
[10]**concert hall:** the place where musicians play music for an audience

home from work, he gave his children a bath, put them to bed, and played piano from 9:00 P.M. until 11:00 P.M. His wife was not happy about his musical obsession, but Tony could not stop. He was certain that music was the reason that he was alive. After a few years, his marriage ended, probably because of his obsession with music.

6   It is now 15 years after Tony was hit by lightning. In spite of what happened to his marriage, Tony believes that music is the best thing that ever happened to him. When he plays his music for other people, he feels wonderful. He says the feeling is like the peaceful yet exciting feeling he got when he almost died. Recently Tony gave his first concert where he played one of his own musical compositions, *Lightning Sonata*.

7   Is there a medical reason for Tony's sudden love of music? Did something happen to his brain when he was hit by lightning? Or is his new interest in music an **emotional** reaction[11] to almost dying? Tony does not know, but whatever the reason, he feels lucky to have this musical gift.

----

[11]**reaction:** something that you feel or do because of something that has happened or something that someone has said

Identifying Main Ideas

A. Read the question. Circle the letter of the best answer.

1. What is the main idea of the reading?

    a. Tony Cicoria is both a musician and a surgeon.

    b. Tony Cicoria developed a sudden interest in music after he was hit by lightning.

    c. Tony Cicoria's marriage ended because of his obsession with music.

B. Put the events from the story in the correct order. Write 1 for the first thing that happened, 2 for the second thing that happened, and so on.

_____ 1. The doctor did some tests and told Tony he was fine.

_1_ 2. Tony was hit by lightning while making a phone call.

_____ 3. Tony went to see a doctor because he couldn't remember names of people and diseases.

_____ 4. Tony started listening to piano music all the time.

_____ 5. Tony started to have dreams about writing and performing his own piano music.

_____ 6. Tony gave his first piano concert.

_____ 7. Tony started to take piano lessons.

_____ 8. Tony wanted to write down the music he heard in his dreams.

_____ 9. Tony almost died.

_____ 10. Tony's marriage ended.

Identifying Details

Mark the statements T (true) or F (false). Correct the false statements.

_F_ 1. When Tony was hit by lightning, he ~~went~~ *didn't go* to the hospital.

____ 2. Tony had some problems with his memory after he was hit by lightning.

____ 3. Tony's memory problems went away after a short time.

____ 4. Tony already knew how to read and write music when he was hit by lightning.

____ 5. Tony had dreams about being hit by lightning.

____ 6. Tony practiced playing the piano for eight hours every day.

____ 7. Tony's wife was happy about her husband's sudden interest in music.

____ 8. Today, Tony writes and plays his own musical compositions.

Making Inferences

READING SKILL

Writers do not always say everything directly. Sometimes readers need to **make inferences** to understand the writer's meaning. An inference is a logical conclusion based on evidence. An inference is more than a guess because it is based on information from a text. For example, read the following sentences from "A Gift of Music." Pay attention to the shaded sentences.

EXAMPLE

- "The weather was pleasant, but I could see storm clouds in the distance. After the call, I was still holding the receiver when I heard [a] . . . crack and saw a flash of light come out of the phone and hit me in the face."

In this example, the writer does not say directly that Tony was hit by lightning, but you can make that inference because of the shaded information.

Be careful when you make an inference. Make sure that your inference is based on the information in the text. For example, after reading the sentences above, it would *not* be correct to make the inference that Tony held onto the receiver because he was angry with his mother. Nothing in the text could lead you to that conclusion.

Practice

Look at the sentences from the reading on pages 140–141. Make inferences. Circle the letter of the correct answer.

1. He is a very good doctor, and until 1994, his medical career and his family were the most important things in his life. But all of that changed at a payphone in 1994.

    (a.) Today something besides his medical career and his family is very important to Tony.

    b. Tony doesn't care about his medical career or his family anymore.

2. He started to have dreams about music in which he was playing piano in a concert hall, in front of a large audience. The music was not Chopin, however; he was playing one of his own musical compositions.

    a. Tony was a better composer than Chopin.

    b. Tony was interested in composing his own music.

3. There were a lot of people around him, and a woman was performing CPR. He thought that he was dead.

    a. Tony was probably not breathing after the lightning hit him.

    b. The woman was a doctor.

4. He thought that he was dead. Then he was surrounded by a bluish-white light. He remembers a deep feeling of peace. At the same time, he felt very excited about where he was going.

    a. Tony was not afraid of dying.

    b. Tony was unhappy with his life before he was hit by lightning.

FROM READING TO WRITING

Reflecting on the Reading

Discuss the questions in pairs or small groups.

1. Do you think that Tony's sudden obsession with music resulted from a change in his brain or an emotional experience? Can you think of any other explanation?
2. Tony thinks that what happened to him is a gift. Do you agree?
3. Do you know anyone who almost died? If so, was his or her experience similar to Tony's? How did that person's life change after the experience?

Activating Your Vocabulary

Which sentence is closest in meaning to the one with the boldfaced word or phrase? Circle the letter.

1. The birth of my daughter was a very **emotional** moment.
   a. It hurt a lot when my daughter was born.
   b. I had a lot of strong feelings when my daughter was born.

2. There was a lot of **damage** to his heart.
   a. Something happened to his heart, and now there is a problem.
   b. Something happened to his heart, but now he is better.

3. He **has trouble** reading.
   a. He spends a lot of time reading.
   b. Reading is difficult for him.

4. I remember seeing a **flash** of light in the sky.
   a. The sky got lighter and lighter.
   b. There was a sudden light in the sky, and then it was dark again.

5. He found **peace** when he was an old man.
   a. He had many exciting experiences when he was old.
   b. As an old man, he lived a quiet, calm life.

6. This is my favorite **composition**.
   a. I love to write music.
   b. I love this piece of music.

7. The **audience** did not like the music in the play.
   a. The people watching the play did not like the music.
   b. The people playing the music did not like the music.

8. My headache **went away**.
   a. I don't have headaches anymore.
   b. My head stopped hurting.

Read the model paragraph.

MODEL

Magical Music

Twenty five years ago, I had my first experience singing choral music. At that time, a friend of mine invited me to join the local chorus with her. At first I said no because I couldn't read music, but I finally agreed to go to one rehearsal. That night the chorus was practicing Johann Sebastian Bach's *Magnificat*. As soon as they began to sing, I felt a wonderful sense of peace and I wanted to sing that magical music.

WRITING SKILL

Using Adverbs to Show Time

Some adverbs show the time relationship between ideas in two sentences. These adverbs include *after a while*, *afterwards*, *at that time*, *finally*, and *then*. They come at the beginning of a sentence, before the subject. Look at the examples:

EXAMPLES

- He thought that he was dead. **Then** he was surrounded by a bluish-white light.
- We watched the rain outside the window. **After a while**, it stopped.

Practice

Rewrite the sentences in your notebook. Add the adverbs in parentheses. Use commas when necessary.

1. Chopin showed talent when he was a child. People compared him to Mozart and Beethoven. (after a while)

   Chopin showed talent when he was a child. After a while, people compared him to Mozart and Beethoven.

2. Chopin was in love with a few women. He met George Sand, who became a famous woman author. (then)
3. Chopin met George Sand at a party. He did not like her. (at first)
4. Chopin and George Sand had a love affair. He was becoming very ill. (at that time)
5. Chopin and George Sand's love affair lasted ten years. They went their separate ways. (then)
6. Chopin produced many great works of music. He died after many years of sickness. (finally)

Using Time Clauses with *when, after, before, as soon as*

A time clause is a dependent clause. It joins a main clause to make one sentence. The time clause can come before or after the main clause. When the time clause comes first, use a comma. Use the subordinator *when, after, before,* or *as soon as* in a time clause. Look at the examples:

EXAMPLES

┌─────────── TIME CLAUSE ───────────┐ ┌─────────── MAIN CLAUSE ───────────┐

- **When** he got home from work, he gave his children a bath.

┌─────────── MAIN CLAUSE ───────────┐ ┌─────────── TIME CLAUSE ───────────┐

- He gave his children a bath **when** he got home from work.

Practice

A. Combine each pair of sentences with the word in parentheses. The sentences can be written in two ways.

1. Frederick Chopin was seven months old. His family moved to Warsaw, Poland. (when)

   When Frederick Chopin was seven months old, his family moved to Warsaw, Poland.

2. Chopin was seven years old. He composed music and gave concerts. (when)

   _____

   _____

3. Chopin was eleven years old. He performed for Alexander I, the Russian Tsar. (when)

   _____

   _____

4. Chopin died. He wrote over 230 musical works. (before)

   _____

   _____

5. I heard Chopin's music. I wanted to read his biography. (as soon as)

   _____

   _____

146 From Reading to Writing 2

B. Complete the paragraph with the words from the box. Add commas and capital letters where necessary. In some cases, more than one answer is possible.

~~after that~~	at night	the next morning
as soon as	over the next few days	when

The rehearsal ended at 9:30. (1) _____ *After that* _____ I went home and tried to sleep, but I couldn't. I was too emotional. (2) _____ I got up early and drove to the nearest music store to buy a copy of the Bach *Magnificat*. (3) _____ I got home I put it on the stereo. (4) _____ I heard the first note, the world went away, and that same peaceful feeling came over me. (5) _____ I listened to the *Magnificat* day and night. I was obsessed by it. I played it at work. (6) _____ I heard it in my dreams.

Editing

Read the paragraph. Correct the incomplete sentences, and fix the mistakes in capitalization, punctuation, verb tense, and use of adverbs. There are eight mistakes including the example.

Parts of a Whole

When Monday night finally arrived, I was the first person at rehearsal. I was ready to sing, as soon as I heard the first note, everyone around me started to sing. Then, something strange happened. The music doesn't sound the same as it sounded at home. At that moment I understood that the composition was actually many different parts. different people in the chorus were singing different parts. After that I understood my own part in the total sound of the chorus.

Write a paragraph. Follow the steps.

STEP 1   Get ideas.

Choose a topic for your paragraph. Work in pairs. Ask and answer the questions about your topic.

❑ **Topic 1:** How you became interested in a kind of music

❑ **Topic 2:** How you became interested in a hobby or skill (for example, painting, cooking, cars, computer games, sports, etc.)

1. What is your interest? Describe it.
2. When did you first become interested in it?
3. Where did you first become interested in it?
4. How did you learn about it? Did someone tell you about it? Did you read about it?
5. Why are you interested in it?
6. How important is it to you today? How much time do you spend on it?

STEP 2   Organize your ideas.

A. On a piece of paper, draw a chart like this one and take notes about your topic.

WHAT?	WHEN?	WHERE?	HOW?	WHY?	TODAY?

B. Decide how much of the information in the chart to include in your paragraph. Cross out the information that is irrelevant.

C. Decide how to organize the information in your paragraph. For example, will you write about *when* before or after you write about *where*? Number the information in the chart.

D. Write a topic sentence for your paragraph. Then write sentences based on your notes. Use adverbs to show the time order of the events.

STEP 3   **Write your paragraph.**

Write your paragraph. Use the sentences you wrote in Step 2.

STEP 4   **Check your work.**

Read your paragraph. Use the Writing Checklist to look for mistakes, and use the editing symbols on page 192 to mark corrections.

Writing Checklist

❏ Did you write a topic sentence and a concluding sentence?

❏ Did you use adverbs correctly to show the order of events?

❏ Did you use commas and periods correctly?

❏ Did you write complete sentences, with subjects and verbs?

❏ Is your paragraph unified, with no irrelevant sentences?

STEP 5   **Write a final copy.**

Correct your mistakes. Copy your final paragraph and give it to your instructor.

Music and Language

*In this chapter
you will:*

• read about
   perfect pitch

• learn how to
   take notes and
   organize a
   summary

• write a summary

PRE-READING

Discussion

Discuss the questions in pairs or small groups.

1. Look at the photograph of cellist Yo-Yo Ma. Have you ever
   listened to Yo-Yo Ma's music? What country does he come from?
   What instrument does he play?
2. Do you know how to read music? If so, how did you learn?
3. What is your favorite musical instrument?

Vocabulary

Read the boldfaced words and their definitions. Then complete each paragraph with the correct words or phrases.

> **after all:** used to say that something should be remembered or considered because it helps to explain what you have just said
>
> **among:** included in a larger group of people or things
>
> **immediately:** very quickly and without waiting
>
> **compare:** think about how two or more things, people, etc., are different or the same
>
> **depend on:** be affected by something that is not fixed or certain
>
> **include:** If one thing includes another, the second thing is part of the first.
>
> **produce:** make something using a skill or art
>
> **sight:** the ability to see

Yo-Yo Ma is a famous musician. He is (**1**) _____*among*_____ the greatest cello players alive today. He can (**2**) _____ sounds with his cello that no one else can make. After I heard him play the first time, I left the concert hall and went (**3**) _____ to a music store to buy all of his CDs. I was surprised to find that his recordings (**4**) _____ almost every type of music, from classical compositions by Bach to tango music from Argentina.

If you (**5**) _____ a painter and a musician, you will find many similarities. (**6**) _____, both painters and musicians are artists. If their work is good, it makes us think and feel. We use our (**7**) _____ to experience a painting and our ears to experience a piece of music, but both experiences touch our minds and emotions. So why do musicians become musicians and not painters? The answer will (**8**) _____ many things, such as the artist's natural ability and his or her early childhood experiences.

Music and Language

1   Famous cellist[1] Yo-Yo Ma can hear one musical note,[2] such as D sharp (D#), and **immediately** name it. And if you say the name of a musical note, he can sing it perfectly. Where does this special musical ability come from? Why do some people have it, but not others? And is it really special? Is it even musical? Researchers think this special ability to hear musical notes may come from a person's language.

2   In the past, most people believed that only professional musicians had this special ability, called *perfect pitch*. A pitch is a musical note, for example, C sharp (C#). To understand perfect pitch, you can **compare** hearing and **sight**. Most people can see a red apple and name its color. They don't need to compare it to a green apple. They just know that it is red. In the same way, people with perfect pitch can hear one musical note and immediately name it. They don't need to think about it or hear another note to compare it to.

3   Most of us do not think that it takes a special ability to name a color. **After all**, almost everyone can do it. However, perfect pitch is special, isn't it? In fact, new research shows that the answer **depends on** your native language. In the United States and Europe, perfect pitch is rare. Fewer than one person in 10,000 has it. But researchers from the University of California, San Diego, have found something very interesting. **Among** native speakers of certain languages, such as

Mandarin Chinese and Vietnamese, perfect pitch is nine times more common than among native speakers of languages like English or French.

4   But why? Do speakers of those languages have a special musical ability? Not exactly. Mandarin Chinese and Vietnamese are tonal languages. In tonal languages, the pitch, or tone, that you use to say a word can change the word's meaning. For example, in Mandarin there are four tones. The word *ma* means "mother" when you say it in the first tone and "horse" when you say it in the fourth tone. The ability to hear and **produce** different tones correctly is important in tonal languages. It is as important as the difference between a *t* and a *d* to a speaker of English. So perhaps perfect pitch is not a musical ability. Maybe it is a language ability.

5   To test this idea, researchers studied two groups. The first group **included** 88 first-year music students in China. The second group included 115 first-year music students in the United States. The Chinese students were all native speakers of Mandarin, a tonal language. The students in the United States were all native speakers of non-tonal languages, including English.

6   The tests showed some big differences. Sixty percent of the Chinese students who started their musical training when they were four or five years old had perfect pitch. Compare that to just 14 percent of the speakers of non-tonal languages who started their musical training at the same age. For those who started training between the ages of six and seven, 55 percent of the Chinese students had perfect pitch, but only six

---

[1] **cellist:** someone who plays a cello, a big musical instrument that you hold between your knees and play with a bow (a type of stick)
[2] **musical note:** a notation that represents a musical sound

percent of the U.S. group did. And for those beginning between the ages of eight and nine, the figures[3] were 42 percent of the Chinese and zero percent of the U.S. group.

7   What do researchers conclude from these studies? They believe that speakers of tonal languages can hear and produce pitch changes very well because tone is important in their languages. And when speakers of tonal languages have early musical training, this ability develops even more. So in fact, perfect pitch is not a rare musical ability. It is a very common result of learning a tonal language.

----

[3]**figure:** a number or amount

Identifying Main Ideas

A. Read the question. Circle the letter of the best answer.

1. What is the main idea of the reading?
   a. Most speakers of tonal languages study music.
   b. Perfect pitch is a rare musical ability.
   c. Perfect pitch may be a language ability and not a musical ability.

B. Look back at the reading and skim paragraphs 2–7. Write each paragraph number next to the question that it answers. (Do not include paragraph 1.)

_____ 1. How are tonal languages different from non-tonal languages?

_____ 2. What is perfect pitch?

_____ 3. What did the researchers conclude?

_____ 4. Who did the researchers study?

_____ 5. How common is perfect pitch among speakers of both tonal and non-tonal languages?

_____ 6. What did the researchers discover?

Identifying Details

Look at the reading again and complete the chart.

AGE AT START OF MUSICAL TRAINING	PERCENTAGE WITH PERFECT PITCH	
	Tonal Language	Non-Tonal Language
4 to 5	60%	
6 to 7		
8 to 9		

Reflecting on the Reading

Discuss the questions in pairs or small groups.

1. Do you have perfect pitch? Do you know anyone who has perfect pitch?
2. Do you like to sing? Do you think that you have a nice singing voice? Is it easy for you to learn a song?
3. Who is your favorite singer? Why is he or she your favorite?

Activating Your Vocabulary

Complete the paragraph with the words from the box.

after all	compare	including	produces
~~among~~	depends on	immediately	sight

  I know many excellent musicians, but my older brother is
(1) _____*among*_____ the best. He can hear a song one time and play it
back (2) _____. He can also look at the music for a new song
and sing it just by (3) _____. That is, he can read the notes
and sing them perfectly. He can play most musical instruments,
(4) _____ the piano, the guitar, the cello, and the flute. He
also writes his own music. He (5) _____ several new
compositions a month, sometimes more. It (6)_____ how he
feels that month. I am also a musician, but if I (7) _____
myself to him, I have to admit that he is much more talented than I am.
Sometimes I feel bad about that, but most of the time I feel proud because
(8) _____, he is my big brother!

Read the model paragraph.

MODEL

"Music and Language" Summary

The article "Music and Language" is about perfect pitch. People with perfect pitch can hear one musical note and immediately name it. Perfect pitch is rare among speakers of non-tonal languages such as English. Only one in every 10,000 people has perfect pitch. But research shows that among speakers of tonal languages such as Mandarin Chinese, perfect pitch is much more common. Researchers think that more speakers of non-tonal languages develop perfect pitch because pitch changes are so important in their native languages. So maybe perfect pitch is a language ability and not a musical ability after all.

WRITING SKILL

Taking Notes for a Summary

A **summary** is a sentence or paragraph that gives only the main points of something you have read. A summary is written in your own words. Before you write a summary, **take notes** on the important ideas in the reading. One way to organize your notes is by using the six basic question words: *who, what, when, where, how,* and *why.* Look at the notes taken for "'Music and Language' Summary."

WHO	WHAT?	WHERE?	WHEN?	HOW?	WHY?
Yo-Yo Ma	perfect pitch	the U.S.	[no information]	tested 1st-year music students for perfect pitch: native speakers of tonal and non-tonal languages	pitch important in tonal languages, so native speakers good at it
native speakers of tonal and non-tonal languages	perfect pitch more common in tonal languages	China			
language researchers	language ability	University of Southern California, San Diego (researchers)			

Practice

Look at the information in the chart on page 155 and compare it to the information in the model paragraph summary. Cross out the information in the notes that is not included in the model paragraph.

WRITING SKILL

Organizing a Summary

A summary shows how well you understand the reading. When you write a summary, include only the most important information: the main idea and the main supporting points. Do not include details.

Here are some tips for **organizing a summary**:

- In general, a summary of a short article should not be more than one paragraph long.
- Start with a general sentence giving the title, author (if available), and the topic of the reading. Then give the most important information from the reading.
- Remember: Never copy sentences from a reading when you write a summary. Instead, take your own notes about the reading. Then write the summary from your notes.

Practice

A. *Read three summaries of "A Gift of Music" (pages 140–141). As you read, think about which summary is the best.*

Paragraph 1

Tony Cicoria's Gift

"A Gift of Music" is about Tony Cicoria, a doctor who was hit by lightning and then suddenly developed an obsession with music. Before the accident, Tony had no interest in music at all. He didn't know how to read music or play a musical instrument. But after the accident, music became the most important thing in Tony's life. Recently Tony gave his first public piano performance. He played one of his own compositions. Tony doesn't know why he became obsessed with music after his accident, but he is happy that it happened. He thinks that his obsession with music is a gift.

Paragraph 2

The Flash of Lightning

"A Gift of Music" is about a doctor named Tony Cicoria. One day, he was talking to his mother on the phone when he saw a flash of light and heard a loud cracking noise. The next thing he remembers is looking down on his own body on the ground. He thought that he was dead, but he wasn't scared. He felt peaceful. But he didn't die. He wasn't even badly hurt, so he didn't go to the hospital. After his experience, he had some memory problems for a couple of weeks, but he soon got better. Then he started listening to piano music and taking piano lessons. He and his wife got a divorce. Today Tony is still a doctor, but he also writes his own compositions and performs them. One of his compositions is called *Lightning Sonata.*

Paragraph 3

A Life-Changing Experience

Tony Cicoria is a very good doctor, and until 1994, his medical career and his family were the most important things in his life. But all of that changed in 1994 when he was hit by lightning. At first, he felt okay. But then two weeks later, something strange started to happen to Tony. He suddenly became completely obsessed with piano music. This was especially strange because Tony had never been interested in music before. But there was one big problem: He could not read or write music. So Tony started taking piano lessons. Music became the most important thing in his life. Recently Tony gave his first concert. Is there a medical reason for Tony's sudden love of music? Tony does not know, but whatever the reason, he feels lucky to have this musical gift.

B. Check (✔) the information that is true for each summary.

	SUMMARY 1	SUMMARY 2	SUMMARY 3
States the title			
Includes the main idea			
Includes the most important information			
Gives too many details			
Copies sentences from the reading			

C. Write the number of the best summary: _____

D. Compare answers with a partner or as a class.

WRITING ASSIGNMENT

Write a summary of one of the readings listed below. Follow the steps.

1. "Pizza around the World" (page 26)
2. "Ray Charles" (pages 48–49)
3. "Using YouTube" (pages 105–106)

STEP 1   Get ideas.

A. Read the article again. On a piece of paper, draw a chart like the one below and write notes. If there is no information for a question word, leave that space blank.

WHO?	WHAT?	WHERE?	WHEN?	HOW?	WHY?

B. Find a partner who chose the same reading. Compare your notes. Make changes if necessary.

STEP 2   **Organize your ideas.**

A. Check (✔) the information in your notes that you want to include in your summary. Remember, include only the most important information.

B. Complete the first sentence of your summary. Give the title and the topic:

"_____" is about _____.

C. Write sentences about the main points. Use the information you checked in your notes.

D. Write the main idea of the reading:

_____

STEP 3   **Write your paragraph.**

Write your paragraph. Use the sentences you wrote in Step 2.

STEP 4   **Check your work.**

Read your paragraph. Use the writing checklist to look for mistakes, and use the editing symbols on page 192 to mark corrections.

Writing Checklist

❏ Did you use correct paragraph format?

❏ Did you use your own words?

❏ Did you include the main points and the main idea, but not the details?

❏ Did you use connecting words to go from one main idea to the next?

❏ Did you use commas and periods correctly?

STEP 5   **Write a final copy.**

Correct your mistakes. Copy your final paragraph and give it to your instructor.

UNIT EIGHT

Education

From a Distance

*In this chapter
you will:*

- read an article
  about distance
  education

- learn to
  recognize facts
  and opinions

- write an opinion
  paragraph

PRE-READING

Discussion

Discuss the questions in pairs or small groups.

1. Look at the photo. Who are the people? What are they doing?
2. Why do college students choose to live on campus? Why do they choose to live off campus?
3. Where do you prefer to study—at home or at school? Why?
4. What are the advantages (good things) of going to college? Are there any negatives (bad things)?

Vocabulary

Read the boldfaced words and their definitions. Then complete each sentence with the correct word or phrase.

> **benefit:** an advantage or other useful thing that you get from something
>
> **exist:** be in the world
>
> **flexible:** able to change easily
>
> **in order to:** so that something can happen, or so that someone can do something
>
> **option:** something that you can choose to do
>
> **reduce:** make something less than it was before in amount, size, price, etc.
>
> **sign:** something different or unusual that shows what is starting to happen
>
> **typical:** having the usual qualities of a particular person, group, or thing

1. Sandy wants to _____reduce_____ the number of hours she works. Working ten hours a day is too difficult for her.

2. On a _____ weekday, Maria goes to class in the morning and works at night. This is her normal schedule Mondays to Fridays.

3. Rick had the _____ of going to college when he finished high school, but he waited a year so he could work and earn some money first.

4. John has three roommates, so he often studies at the library _____ have a quiet place to study.

5. Some teachers do not let their students turn in work late. Others are _____, allowing students to have extra time.

6. During the last week of classes, college students can look very tired. This is a _____ that they are studying all night for their final exams.

7. Two kinds of high schools _____ in the United States: public schools and private schools.

8. When you go to college, you learn a lot of new things. Another _____ is that you meet many interesting people.

From a Distance

1   Samantha Robinson turns on her computer and checks her e-mail. Then she watches a couple of YouTube videos that a friend told her about. Finally, she decides to find out what her next assignment will be in her European History class. She goes to her university's web page and signs in. She sees a message from her professor. She joins a chat room and notices that eight other students are there, too. They begin to discuss the professor's assignment and share ideas. Some of these students live on campus. Others live an hour away. A few live in a different country. Samantha's situation is more **typical** than you might think. More and more college students are deciding to take distance education, or DE, classes. DE classes let students take college courses from home using their computer and the Internet. Taking a distance education course is a smart decision for many reasons.

2   First of all, taking a DE class can save students money. If students don't have to drive to school, they **reduce** the amount of money they spend on gasoline and parking. As gas prices increase, this is an important consideration.[1] Furthermore, students with children do not have to put their children in daycare **in order to** take classes. Parents can save hundreds of dollars a month if they don't use daycare. One expense[2] of a DE class is the cost of a computer. However, today you can buy a computer for less than five hundred dollars. Purchasing[3] a computer is money well spent. After a year of traditional classes, you would probably pay more than five hundred dollars on gas and parking alone.

3   Another **benefit** of DE classes is having many course and school **options**. Most U.S. universities offer online[4] classes. More than one-third of American colleges allow you to earn a degree from home. In addition, there are thousands of DE classes available every semester from schools all around the world. This means that a person living in Tokyo could take a class at New York University, and a New Yorker could take a class at the University of London—all without really being there. For people who don't live near any university at all, DE classes are even more helpful. For them, DE classes open up a door to higher education that never **existed** before. DE can bring people and schools close together no matter how far apart they are.

4   Finally, the best part of DE classes is their **flexible** schedule. You don't have to "be on-time" to class. You decide when to work on your assignments, listen to lectures, and take exams. People who like mornings can do their assignments early. People who work better at night can wait until after dinner. You can even take exams at midnight in your pajamas if you want! As usual, there are due dates.[5] But you don't have to follow a strict[6] schedule every day like you do in a traditional class. This is

---

[1] **consideration:** careful thought about something
[2] **expense:** money that you have to spend on something

[3] **purchasing:** buying something
[4] **online:** using the Internet
[5] **due date:** the date by which an assignment must be finished
[6] **strict:** expecting people to obey the rules or do what you say

perfect for people who can't take classes on campus because of their work hours. It also benefits parents who need to be at home to take care of their children. These parents can still take a class.

5   DE classes can make people's lives easier. They are a good option for students who like to learn on computers. They also teach students to be more independent learners, which is an important skill. The number of people taking DE classes is continually growing. As the number of DE students grows, the world seems to get smaller. Distance education is bringing schools and students closer together. It is just another **sign** that we live in a global[7] society.

----

[7]**global:** affecting or including the whole world

Identifying Main Ideas

Read each question. Circle the letter of the best answer.

1. What is the main idea of the reading?

 a. Many universities offer DE classes.

 b. A lot of people take DE classes.

 c. Taking DE classes is a good idea.

2. What is the main idea of paragraph 2?

 a. You can take DE classes from home.

 b. DE classes can save students money.

 c. DE classes require a computer.

3. What is the main idea of paragraph 3?

 a. Some people don't live near a university.

 b. American colleges offer DE classes.

 c. DE classes give people many options.

4. The reading can be best described as _____.

 a. a description of DE programs

 b. an opinion piece about DE classes

 c. a history of computers and education

Identifying Details

*Mark the statements **T** (true) or **F** (false). Correct the false statements.*

_F_ 1. It is ~~hard~~ *easy* to find a computer for less than $1,000.

____ 2. DE classes can save parents time and money.

____ 3. More than two-thirds of U.S. colleges offer online degrees.

____ 4. If you don't live near a university, DE classes are not very helpful.

____ 5. Students in a DE class can take exams at midnight.

____ 6. The number of people taking DE classes is increasing.

____ 7. The University of London offers some online classes.

____ 8. When you take a DE class, you do not communicate with the other students.

READING SKILL

Recognizing Facts and Opinions

A **fact** is something that is true. You cannot agree or disagree with a fact. Facts tell about a real situation.

EXAMPLES

- In the United States, more than one-third of American colleges allow you to earn a degree from home.
- There are thousands of DE classes available every semester from schools all around the world.

An **opinion** is a belief or feeling about something. You can agree or disagree with an opinion. Opinion statements often use words such as *good*, *bad*, *best*, *seems to*, *should*, and *in my opinion*. You can also add description words such as *smart*, *perfect*, and *important*.

EXAMPLES

- DE classes are a good option for students who like to learn through the Internet.
- As the number of DE students grows, the world seems to get smaller.

Practice

Mark the statements from the reading F (fact) or O (opinion). Compare your answers with a partner's.

_F_ 1. DE classes let students take college courses from home using their computer and the Internet.

_____ 2. Taking a distance education course is a smart decision for many reasons.

_____ 3. Today you can buy a computer for less than five hundred dollars.

_____ 4. Purchasing a computer is money well spent.

_____ 5. The best part of DE classes is their flexible schedule.

_____ 6. The number of people taking DE classes is continually growing.

FROM READING TO WRITING

Reflecting on the Reading

Discuss the questions in pairs or small groups.

1. Would you like to take a distance education class? Why or why not?
2. The author of "From a Distance" feels that the world is getting smaller. Do you agree or disagree? Why?

Activating Your Vocabulary

Complete the sentences with the words from the box.

benefit	flexible	option	sign
exist	~~in order to~~	reduce	typical

1. Paul is going to medical school ___*in order to*___ become a doctor.

2. Finding higher-paying jobs is a(n) _____ of getting a college degree.

3. The first online universities didn't _____ until the late 1980s.

4. Distance education classes are a(n) _____ that many colleges now offer.

(continued)

5. Taking four or five classes is _____ for college students who study full-time.

6. Asking questions in class is a(n) _____ that you are paying attention.

7. Jonas took distance education classes because he wanted a(n) _____ class schedule.

8. The teacher decided to _____ the amount of homework for tomorrow's class.

WRITING

Read the model paragraph.

MODEL

Dorm Life

Students should live in a dorm for three important reasons. First of all, living on campus is very convenient. It is easy to visit the library to do research, and it takes only minutes to get to class. Second, being in a dorm is fun. Sometimes dorms have parties and activities for students. These are good ways to meet other people, and they give students a nice break from studying. Finally, dorms are very safe. Only students who live there can enter. Also, there are usually school police around to make sure the area around the dorm is safe. College students have many options for student housing, but living in a dorm is one of the best.

Organizing an Opinion Paragraph

An **opinion paragraph** explains a personal belief that you have. An effective opinion paragraph should:
- have a topic sentence that states your opinion about the topic
- give reasons and examples to support your opinion
- have a concluding sentence that restates your opinion

Look at the outline on the next page. Notice how "Dorm Life" includes all three of these things to make an effective opinion paragraph.

I. **Topic Sentence:** Students should live in a dorm for three important reasons.

  A. **Reason 1:** First of all, living on campus is very convenient.

  Example: It is easy to visit the library to do research, and it takes only minutes to get to class.

  B. **Reason 2:** Second, living in a dorm is fun.

  Example: Sometimes dorms have parties and activities for students. These are good ways to meet other people, and they give students a nice break from studying.

  C. **Reason 3:** Finally, dorms are very safe.

  Examples: Only students who live there can enter.

  Also, there are usually school police around to make sure the area around the dorm is safe.

II. **Concluding Sentence:** College students have several options for student housing, but living in a dorm is one of the best.

Practice

Look at the outline. Add reasons and examples to support the topic sentence. Then write a concluding sentence.

Taking Traditional Classes

I. Topic Sentence: <u>*Taking classes on campus is the best option for students.*</u>

  A. Reason 1: <u>*Students get to know the teacher better.*</u>
  Example: <u>*They can see what the teacher's personality is like.*</u>

  B. Reason 2: _____
  Example: _____

  C. Reason 3: _____
  Example: _____

II. Concluding Sentence:

  _____

  _____

WRITING SKILL

Using *in order to* and *so that*

The phrases *in order to* and *so that* show purpose, or a reason, why something happens.

EXAMPLES

⌐ PURPOSE ⌐

- Paul is going to college **in order to** get a degree.

⌐ PURPOSE ⌐

- Jackie takes evening classes **so that** she can work during the day.

In the first sentence, Paul's purpose or reason is to get a degree. In the second sentence, Jackie's purpose or reason is to work during the day. Note that *in order to* comes before the base form of a verb, and *so that* comes before a subject + verb.

EXAMPLES

- I left my house early **in order to** <u>be</u> at class on time.
- My friend and I met after school **in order to** <u>study</u> for the test.
- I left my house early **so that** <u>I was</u> at class on time.
- My friend and I met after school **so that** <u>we could study</u> for the test.

Practice

Complete the sentences with **in order to** *or* **so that.**

1. Teachers take attendance _____*in order to*_____ know who is present and who is absent.

2. John is going to college full-time _____ he can finish in four years.

3. Students see tutors _____ get extra help with assignments.

4. Thomas sat in the front row _____ he was able to hear the teacher.

5. Colleges offer students financial aid _____ they can afford college.

6. Erin went to see her teacher _____ find out when her paragraph was due.

Editing

Read the paragraph. Correct the incomplete sentences, and fix the mistakes in capitalization, punctuation, and subject-verb agreement. There are eight mistakes including the example.

Benefits of a Small College

There are important benefits of going to a small *c* College. Small colleges usually has smaller classes. For example, 20 to 30 students in a class. Therefore, it was easier to talk to the professor. Also you get to know your classmates better. Second, small colleges are easier to walk around and you can get to the library or the cafeteria in minutes. Another benefit is that they make you comfortable. Because you feel like you are part of a big family. These are the reason why I go to a small college.

WRITING ASSIGNMENT

Write a paragraph. Follow the steps.

STEP 1   **Get ideas.**

A. Choose a topic statement for your paragraph. Decide whether you agree or disagree with the topic statement.

❑ **Topic 1:** Taking classes on campus is the best option for students.

❑ **Topic 2:** Students should work and take classes at the same time.

B. List reasons with examples to show why you agree or disagree with the statement.

  1. Reason: _____

      Example: _____

  2. Reason: _____

      Example: _____

  3. Reason: _____

      Example: _____

STEP 2   Organize your ideas.

On a piece of paper, make an outline. Use one of the topic sentences to begin your paragraph. Look at the reasons you listed in Step 1 and put them in order of importance, with the most important reason last. Decide which examples you will use to support your reasons.

STEP 3   Write your paragraph.

Write your paragraph. Follow the outline you made in Step 2.

STEP 4   Check your work.

Read your paragraph. Use the writing checklist to look for mistakes, and use the editing symbols on page 192 to mark corrections.

Writing Checklist

❑ Did you write a topic sentence and a concluding sentence?

❑ Did you include at least three reasons to support your opinion?

❑ Did you include examples to support your reasons?

❑ Did you write complete sentences, with subjects and verbs?

❑ Did you use correct punctuation?

STEP 5   Write a final copy.

Correct your mistakes. Copy your final paragraph and give it to your instructor.

A Healthy Education

PRE-READING

Discussion

Discuss the questions in pairs or small groups.

1. What kinds of food do you eat at home and at school?
2. Does going to school make people eat better or worse? Explain.
3. Name different ways students can keep themselves healthy.

Vocabulary

Read the sentences. Match the boldfaced words with the definitions in the box.

___c___ 1. Doctors **earn** more money than teachers, but they go to school longer.

_____ 2. Sarah wanted to **enhance** her hair color with red highlights.

_____ 3. Researchers are trying to **discover** why some people do better in school than others. They want to find reasons for the differences.

_____ 4. Many things can affect where people go to college, including the size and location of the school. Another important **factor** is how much it costs.

_____ 5. When students attend class, they **are** more **likely to** understand the information.

_____ 6. Jackson took a big **risk** yesterday. He drove his car very fast in order to get to class on time. Luckily, he didn't get a speeding ticket.

_____ 7. There was a terrible snowstorm last night. **Consequently**, all schools and businesses are closed today.

_____ 8. When Linda started her new job, she made $30,000 a year. After working for ten years, her **income** increased to $45,000.

---

    a. find something hidden, unknown
    b. the money that you get from working
    c. get money for the work you do
    d. the chance that something bad might happen
    e. probably happen or be true
    f. as a result
    g. become better, or make something better
    h. one of many things that affects a situation

A Healthy Education

1   People often say that education is the "key to success." Just as a key opens a door, education opens doors to more jobs and a better future. In the United States, a person with a high school degree will **earn** about $1 million during his or her working years. A college graduate will make $1.6 million. People who study more than four years of college will earn around $2 million. Many people think that the more educated you are, the better job you will have. However, did you know that having more education may help make you healthier, too? According to some scientists, going to college can **enhance** both your physical and mental[1] health.

2   Research shows that having a higher level of education is correlated with[2] a longer life. Researcher Adriana Lleras-Muney studies longevity. She **discovered** that people live eighteen months longer for each year of school they finish. In addition, high school graduates live nine years longer than high school dropouts.[3] Going to college improves a person's longevity even more. Scientists believe that college graduates live longer because they have healthier lifestyles. But why are they healthier?

3   One **factor** seems to be that college grads often make healthier choices. For instance, they **are** less **likely to** smoke. In the United States 34 percent of smokers do not have a high school degree. In contrast, only

10 percent of college graduates smoke. As a result, college-educated individuals report fewer chronic[4] diseases, such as emphysema[5] and heart disease.

4   College-educated individuals also seem to have healthier eating habits. Research suggests that they drink less coffee and eat more fruits and vegetables. As a result, they **are** at **less risk** of being obese.[6] In 2007, 39 percent of American high school graduates were obese. In contrast, only 24 percent of college graduates were obese. These numbers suggest that there is a connection between education and health.

5   Finishing college is not only connected with better physical health. Scientists say that graduates have fewer mental problems, too. People with more education seem to have less depression.[7] In addition, college-educated people have less memory loss when they get older. Dr. Edward Coffey studies the effects of aging on the brain. As you age, your brain begins to weaken. This can cause memory problems. However, "educated brains" fight memory loss better, says Dr. Coffey. He and other scientists believe that education "exercises the brain" and keeps it active. When your brain is active, you remember more, you stay healthier, and you live longer.

(continued)

[1]**mental:** relating to the mind
[2]**correlated with:** when two things show a connection or relationship. It does not necessarily prove that one thing <u>causes</u> another thing.
[3]**dropout:** someone who leaves school or college without finishing it

[4]**chronic:** a chronic disease or illness continues for a long time and cannot be cured
[5]**emphysema:** a serious disease that affects the lungs
[6]**obese:** very fat in a way that is unhealthy
[7]**depression:** a feeling of great sadness that sometimes makes you unable to live normally

6   Are educated people also healthier because they can get better jobs and earn more money? **Income** can affect a person's health. For example, people with little money cannot afford to pay for health insurance; **consequently**, they might not go to the doctor when they are sick. However, scientists have discovered that education often has more influence on health than income does. When two people earn similar incomes, the person with more education will usually be healthier, says researcher Lleras-Muney.

7   Of course, education does not guarantee good health. There are many unhealthy college graduates. Many people who never go to college are healthy and live long lives, too.

The truth is that staying healthy is not as simple as just going to college. Many factors affect health. Some you can control, like eating habits and exercise. Other factors you cannot control, like family history.

8   Still, some researchers think that going to college affects your health positively. It is linked to lower smoking rates, better eating habits, and improved memory. So although there is no secret recipe for long life, getting a college degree may be one of the secret ingredients.[7]

----

[7]**ingredients:** foods that you use to make a particular dish; qualities that help to do or get something

Identifying Main Ideas

Match each paragraph with its main idea.

  _b_   1. paragraph 2

_____ 2. paragraph 3

_____ 3. paragraph 4

_____ 4. paragraph 5

_____ 5. paragraph 6

a. College graduates are more likely to make healthier choices.
b. Having more education is connected with the length of a person's life.
c. College graduates often have fewer mental problems.
d. A higher income can improve a person's health.
e. College graduates have healthier habits.

Identifying Details

Mark the statements **T** *(true) or* **F** *(false). Correct the false statements.*

_____ 1. High school graduates live nine months longer than high school dropouts.

_____ 2. In the United States 34 percent of smokers do not have a college degree.

_____ 3. Some scientists believe that college graduates live longer because they have healthier lifestyles.

_____ 4. Dr. Coffey discovered that "educated brains" fight depression better.

_____ 5. Adriana Lleras-Muney found that income affects health more than education does.

FROM READING TO WRITING

Reflecting on the Reading

Discuss the questions in pairs or small groups.

1. Why do some people not finish high school? Are there ways to stop this? Explain.
2. Name different ways people can keep their brain "active" after they finish school. In which ways do you prefer to keep your mind active?
3. This reading discusses how college may influence people's health and their habits. Consider your high school experience. Did it affect your health or habits? For example:
   - eating habits
   - social behavior and relationships

Activating Your Vocabulary

A. Complete the sentences with the words from the box. Capitalize the words when necessary.

are likely to	discover	enhance	income
consequently	~~earn~~	factor	risk

1. People who go to college usually _____earn_____ more money than people who don't.

2. Students can _____ their health by exercising.

3. People who have a low _____ have difficulty paying for health insurance.

4. Reading history books helps you _____ many facts.

5. Scientists think that going to college is one _____ that can affect your health.

6. Non-smokers have less _____ of getting heart disease.

7. Education exercises the brain. _____, many older people take classes to keep their brains healthy.

8. College graduates _____ have fewer mental problems, which might help reduce the risk of depression.

B. Complete the paragraph with words from Exercise A. Capitalize the words when necessary.

College has many benefits, but it can cause stress. Students have a lot of deadlines, so they (**1**) _____ stay up late, which increases stress. Another (**2**) _____ causing stress is that some students work jobs to (**3**) _____ money for expenses. This gives them less time to meet their deadlines. They also are at more (**4**) _____ for stress if they are living far away from family. (**5**) _____, it is especially important for them to stay healthy by eating well and exercising.

Read the model cause paragraph.

MODEL

Reasons Students Join Clubs

There are many reasons for the popularity of school clubs. First, students often join a club to practice a skill or sport. For example, chess and karate club members improve their abilities by practicing daily. Second, students sometimes join clubs because they think it will help them get into university. Universities want students to participate in clubs, like the debate club. Most important, students join clubs to make friends and have fun.

Read the model effect paragraph.

MODEL

Joining a Student Club

Being a part of a school club can have many positive effects on students. First, clubs can make students better leaders because they run the clubs and make important decisions about its activities and members. Second, clubs make students feel closer to their school community. Club members often work with teachers, and clubs have many events for the school such as concerts. Overall, clubs help students feel positively about themselves.

WRITING SKILL

Writing a Cause Paragraph or an Effect Paragraph

A cause paragraph explains why something happens. An effect paragraph explains the effects or the results of something. The chart on page 180 shows causes for the first model paragraph.

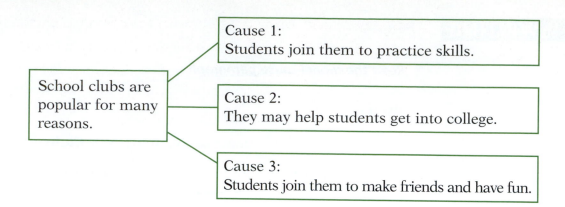

Cause 1:
Students join them to practice skills.

Cause 2:
They may help students get into college.

Cause 3:
Students join them to make friends and have fun.

School clubs are popular for many reasons.

When you write a paragraph on causes or effects, you need to explain them in detail so that your ideas are clear.

Practice

A. Look back at the effect paragraph "Joining a Student Club" on page 179. Draw a chart like this one in your notebook. Write two effects from the paragraph in the boxes.

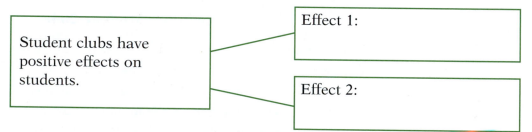

Student clubs have positive effects on students.

Effect 1:

Effect 2:

B. Discuss the topics with a partner. Write two causes and two effects.

1. a. Why do students not get enough sleep?

   Cause 1: *They stay up late studying for tests.*

   Cause 2: _____

   b. What effects does too little sleep have on students?

   Effect 1: _____

   Effect 2: _____

2. a. Why do people choose to study in a foreign country?

   Cause 1: _____

   Cause 2: _____

   b. What effects does speaking a foreign language have on people's lives?

   Effect 1: _____

   Effect 2: _____

C. Match each cause or effect with the correct explanation in the box.

___c___ 1. Dropping out of high school affects your work.

_____ 2. Financial aid helps college students pay for books.

_____ 3. Joining a sports team at school is good for you.

_____ 4. Many people go to community college because they want a two-year degree.

_____ 5. Teachers give tests to help them understand their students better.

> a. Getting a community-college degree gives them more job options.
> b. Tests help teachers see what their students know and don't know.
> c. If you do not finish high school, you will have fewer job options.
> d. Because books are very expensive, many students need help buying them.
> e. You exercise regularly, which benefits your health.

WRITING SKILL

Using Logical Connectors to Show Cause and Effect

Cause Markers

Because of and *as a result of* are prepositional phrases that introduce a cause. They are followed by a noun. They can be at the beginning or in the middle of a sentence.

EXAMPLES

- ⌐ CAUSE ⌐
  As a result of/Because of the rain, the game was canceled.

- ⌐CAUSE⌐
  The game was canceled **because of/as a result of** the rain.

Put a comma after the noun when the phrases are used at the beginning of the sentence.

Effect Markers

As a result, *consequently*, and *therefore* are adverbs that introduce an effect. They are followed by a complete sentence.

EXAMPLES

- ⌐———— EFFECT ————⌐
  It rained. **Consequently/As a result/Therefore,** the game was canceled.

- ⌐———— EFFECT ————⌐
  It rained; **consequently/as a result/therefore,** the game was canceled.

Place effect markers after a period or a semicolon and follow them with a comma.

Practice

Complete the sentences with the words from the box. Capitalize the words when necessary.

as a result as a result of	because of consequently	therefore

1. John went to bed late last night; ___*consequently*___, he is tired today.

2. _____ the thunderstorm, the electricity went out.

3. Janice wants to be a vet. _____, she needs to take biology.

4. Many people don't go to private schools _____ the high cost of tuition.

5. Jennifer learned Spanish in high school; _____, she doesn't need to take it in college.

Editing

Read the paragraph. Correct the incomplete sentences, and fix the mistakes in capitalization, punctuation, and subject-verb agreement. There are eight mistakes including the example.

Why Students Drop Out of College

Student *s* drop out of college for different reasons. One factor is money. College cost a lot. Books and tuition is expensive, as a result some students can't afford to stay in school. In addition some students find it difficult to study and work at the same time. Because they need money to pay for school. They sometimes have to work more. Therefore they might miss classes, get behind, and want to stop. Luckily, college will always be there if you have to leave. You can go back whenever you want.

WRITING ASSIGNMENT

Write a paragraph. Follow the steps.

STEP 1 **Get ideas.**

Choose a topic for your paragraph. List three causes or effects to discuss in your paragraph about your topic.

❑ **Topic 1:** Why students miss class

❑ **Topic 2:** The effects that missing class has on students

Cause 1 or Effect 1: _____

Cause 2 or Effect 2: _____

Cause 3 or Effect 3: _____

STEP 2 **Organize your ideas.**

A. Write a topic sentence for your paragraph:

_____

B. On a piece of paper, make an outline like the one below. Choose ideas from Step 1 that explain your three causes or effects in more detail.

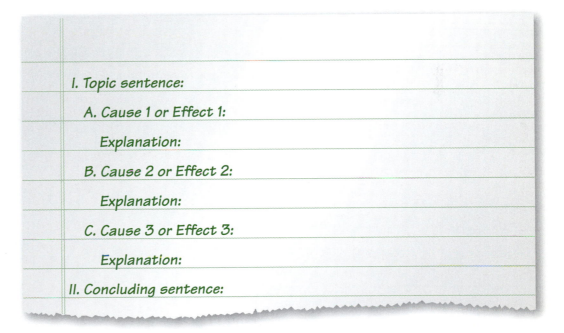

I. Topic sentence:

   A. Cause 1 or Effect 1:

     Explanation:

   B. Cause 2 or Effect 2:

     Explanation:

   C. Cause 3 or Effect 3:

     Explanation:

II. Concluding sentence:

STEP 3 **Write your paragraph.**

Write your paragraph. Follow the outline you made in Step 2.

Check your work.

Read your paragraph. Use the writing checklist to look for mistakes, and use the editing symbols on page 192 to mark corrections.

> ### Writing Checklist
> ❑ Did you write a topic sentence?
> ❑ Did you include three different causes or effects?
> ❑ Did you explain each cause and effect in detail?
> ❑ Did you use cause-effect markers in your paragraph?
> ❑ Did you write a concluding sentence?

STEP 5 **Write a final copy.**

Correct your mistakes. Copy your final paragraph and give it to your instructor.

Grammar Reference

A. Simple Present

The simple present is used to describe regular activities, facts, opinions, or ownership.

1. The Verb *be*

The simple present of *be* has three forms: *am, are, is*. In the negative, *not* comes after the verb.*

FORM/EXAMPLE	MEANING
I **am** always hungry in the morning. I **am not** hungry at noon if I eat a big breakfast.	A regular activity or habit
You **are** never late for breakfast. You **are not** late to lunch, either.	
We **are** almost ready to eat. We **are not** thirsty.	A fact
The bread **is** on the table. The coffee **is not** ready yet.	
The eggs **are** on the stove. The plates **are not** on the table.	

* Negative forms can be shortened: *I am not* = *I'm not. You are not* = *You're not* or *You aren't. We are not* = *We're not* or *We aren't. He is not* = *He's not* or *He isn't. They are not* = *They're not* or *They aren't.*

2. Other Verbs

The simple present of other verbs use the same form for all subjects except *he/she/it*.*

FORM/EXAMPLE	MEANING
Students often **sit** at outside tables to eat their lunch. Usually they **do not sit** on the benches.	A regular activity or habit
The cafeteria **has** excellent service. It **does not serve** pizza. The cook **takes** orders and **prepares** food quickly. The cook **does not talk** very much.	A fact
I **love** pancakes. I **do not like** toast.	An opinion or preference
You **prefer** coffee rather than tea. You **do not like** a cold drink in the morning.	
We **have** a nice, big kitchen for preparing meals. We **don't have** a table in our kitchen.	Ownership

* Negative forms with a *he/she/it* subject have **does not** (or **doesn't**) before the verb.
 Negative forms for other subjects have **do not** (or **don't**) before the verb.

B. Simple Past

The simple past is used to describe situations or activities that began and ended in the past.

1. The Verb *be*

The simple past of *be* has two forms: **was, were**. In the negative, **not** comes after the verb.*

FORM/EXAMPLE
I **was** very tired yesterday. I **wasn't** in a party mood.
You **were** a beautiful baby.
We **were** in the front row the last time.
The crowd **was** large.
The parents **were** happy, but their children **weren't**.

* Negative forms can be shortened: **was not** = **wasn't**, **were not** = **weren't**.

2. Regular Verbs

The simple past of regular verbs is formed by adding *-d* or *-ed* to the simple form of the verb. In the negative, **did not** (or **didn't**) comes before the simple form of the verb.

FORM/EXAMPLE
I **loved** the party.
You **looked** very nice in your new suit.
We **enjoyed** holding the new babies. The babies **didn't cry** until the end of the day.
The food **tasted** delicious.
The guests **thanked** the parents for inviting them.

3. Irregular Verbs

The simple past of irregular verbs have different forms. In the negative, **did not** (or **didn't**) comes before the simple form of the verb.

FORM/EXAMPLE
I **ate** some cake, but I **didn't eat** anything else.
You **took** a lot of photos of the family.
We **spent** several hours at our friends' house.
Everyone **had** a chance to see all four babies together.
The babies **slept** through most of the party.

C. Simple Future

There are several ways to talk about future actions in English: one is to use *will*, another one is to use *be going to*.

1. *Will*

Will is used before the simple form of the verb.* In the negative, *will not* (or *won't*) are used.

FORM/EXAMPLE
I **will take** a vacation on a train across Canada next month. I **won't be** at work.
My vacation **will begin** on July 7, but the train **won't leave** my hometown until July 8.
We **will have** a sleeping car on the train. We **will not watch** one minute of television the whole time!

* This form can be shortened: *I will* = *I'll*. *We will* = *we'll*.

2. *Be going to*

Be going to is used before the simple form of the verb. In the negative, *not* comes after the form of *be*.*

FORM/EXAMPLE
I **am going to see** mountains, lakes, and animals from my train window. **I'm not going to think** about the city or my work.
You **are going to** miss me while I am gone. You **aren't going to be** lonely, are you?
We **are going to eat** all our meals on the train. We **aren't going to cook** or clean our rooms.
The train **is going to** travel across Canada. **It's not going to pick up** more passengers.
The train attendants **are going to tell** us about all the interesting sites along the way. They **aren't going to get** much rest during our trip.

* Negative forms can be shortened (see the simple present of *be*).

D. Imperative

The imperative is used to give commands, directions, advice, or requests.

The imperative is the simple form of the verb without a subject. "You" is the subject, but the word **_you_** is not included in the sentence. In the negative, **_do not_** (or **_don't_**) comes before the simple form of the verb.

FORM/EXAMPLE
Set your goals.
Don't forget them.
Be confident in yourself.
Don't be afraid.

E. Future Real Conditional

The future real conditional is used to explain what will happen under certain conditions.

The _if_ clause shows a condition, and the main clause shows the possible future result of that condition. In the _if_ clause the present tense of the verb is used, and _will_ + the simple tense form is used in the main clause.

FORM/EXAMPLE
It it rains, **I'll stay** home.
I will stay home if it rains.

Punctuation and Capitalization

PUNCTUATION MARK	USE	EXAMPLE
.	Place a period at the end of a statement.	The Gauna family moved to New York last year.
?	Place a question mark at the end of a question.	How many children do Enrique and Andrea Gauna have?
!	Place an exclamation point at the end of a command or a statement that shows strong feeling.	They have six children. That's a lot!
,	Use a comma to indicate a short pause between ideas in a sentence. Follow the rules below. 1. Use commas to list three or more nouns, adjectives, verbs, or phrases. 2. Use commas before and after phrases that describe a person or thing. 3. Use a comma before a conjunction (*and, but, or, so*) that joins main clauses (clauses with a subject and verb) in a compound sentence. 4. Use a comma after a subordinate clause (a group of words that express only part of an idea and begins with *after, although, because, before, if, since, unless, until, when, while*).	On Friday, Saturday, and Sunday Andrea works from 8:00 to 5:00. Enrique, Andrea's husband, is from Puerto Rico. • Enrique has twin brothers, **and** he loves them very much. • Andrea wants to go to California for vacation, **but** Enrique wants to go to Florida. **Before** Andrea went to work, she took her children to school.

PUNCTUATION MARK	USE	EXAMPLE
" "	Use quotation marks to show the exact words that someone said or wrote.	Her son Julio said, "I have soccer practice after school today."
:	Use a colon before a list of items.	Julio plays three sports: soccer, baseball, and basketball.
;	Use a semicolon to separate two related clauses.	His sister Ana doesn't play any sports; she plays the piano.
'	Use an apostrophe in the situations below. 1. Use an apostrophe before or after *s* to show that something belongs or is related to someone. 2. Use an apostrophe to show that a letter has been left out in a contraction.	Andrea is driving Enrique**'s** truck today because her car won't start. She does**n't** like to drive his truck.
L	*Capitalize* means to begin a word with a capital letter. Capitalize words in the following situations: 1. Capitalize the first word of every sentence. 2. Capitalize the pronoun *I*. 3. Capitalize proper nouns (names of people, places, and things).	**T**hey love living in New York City. They like it, but **I** don't. I want to move to **S**eattle.

Editing Symbols

TO	USE THIS	EXAMPLE
add something	$\wedge$	We ate rice, bean, and corn.
delete something	ℬ	We ate rice, beans, and corns.
start a new paragraph	¶	¶We ate rice, beans, and corn.
add a comma	$\wedge$	We ate rice, beans and corn.
add a period	⊙	We ate rice, beans, and corn⊙
switch letters or words	∼	We ate rice, baens, and corn.
change to a capital letter	≡	we ate rice, beans, and corn.
change to a lowercase letter	/	WE ate rice, beans, and corn.

Target Vocabulary

*Coxhead's *Academic Word List* (2000)
**Dilin Liu's *The Most Frequently Used American English Idioms* (2003)

UNIT 1
(Chapters 1 & 2)

adjust*
advice
alone
challenge*
cooperate*
couple*
expect
expensive
financial*
increase
practical
quit
rare
relative
rewarding
temporary*

UNIT 2
(Chapters 3 & 4)

delicious
approximately*
audience
celebrity
generation*
gradually
hit
influence
ingredient
international

percent*
poisonous
profession
recipe
snack
strange

UNIT 3
(Chapters 5 & 6)

admire
aware*
brain
career
confused
create*
disability
encourage
in spite of
lazy
make sense**
overcome
struggle
survive*
take advantage of**
upset

UNIT 4
(Chapters 7 & 8)

anniversary
boarded
luxurious

elegant
explored
magnificent
scenery
keep in touch**
surrounded
location*
spectacular
trade
opportunity
diversity*
multicultural
worth

UNIT 5
(Chapters 9 & 10)

advertisement
afterward
communication*
complained
deal with**
entertain
familiar
invited
last
lonely
look forward to**
message
process*
program
spread
technology*

UNIT 6
(Chapters 11 & 12)

attracted
characteristics
estimate*
expert
figure out**
get to
health
improve
original
quality
recently
research*
responses*
satisfied
tradition*
turned out

UNIT 7
(Chapters 13 & 14)

after all**
among
audience
compare
compositions
damage
depends on
emotional
flash
have trouble
immediately
include
peace
produce
sight
went away

UNIT 8
(Chapters 15 & 16)

are likely to
benefit*
consequently*
discover
earn
enhance
exist
factor*
flexible*
in order to**
income
option*
reduce
risk
sign
typica

Photo Credits

Cover Cloud Nine Productions/CORBIS; **Page 1** Shutterstock; **Page 2** © Kate Powers/Getty Images; **Page 12** iStockphoto; **Page 23** (*left*) iStockphoto, (*right*) iStockphoto; **Page 24** iStockphoto; **Page 35** © Getty Images; **Page 45** Shutterstock; **Page 46** © Reuters/Corbis; **Page 57** © Roger Ressmeyer/CORBIS; **Page 67** Shutterstock; **Page 68** Shutterstock; **Page 73** Shutterstock; **Page 77** Shutterstock; **Page 80** iStockphoto; **Page 85** Shutterstock; **Page 91** Shutterstock; **Page 92** iStockphoto; **Page 103** Shutterstock; **Page 113** Ken Chernus/Getty Images; **Page 114** Jetta Productions; **Page 126** (*left*) Shutterstock, (*right*) Shutterstock; **Page 137** Dreamstime; **Page 138** Lebrecht Music & Arts; **Page 146** © Hulton-Deutsch Collection/CORBIS; **Page 150** World Economic Forum/Swiss_Image/Wikipedia.org; **Page 161** Shutterstock; **Page 162** Superstock; **Page 173** Shutterstock.

Index

Writing

Cause paragraph, 179
Concluding sentence, 53
Connectors, 109
Descriptive details, 75
Effect paragraph, 179
Irrelevant sentences, 98
Narrative, 72
Opinion paragraph, 168
Outline for an opinion
    paragraph, 169
Paragraph with supporting
    sentences, 40
Paragraph with reasons, 62
Paragraph with time clauses, 85
Paragraph with topic sentence
    and controlling idea, 31
Summary, 155
Supporting sentences, 40
Topic sentence, 40
Unified paragraph, 98

Writing Skills

Developing a paragraph with
    supporting sentences, 40
Organizing a summary, 156
Organizing an opinion
    paragraph, 168
Organizing by order of
    importance, 108
Taking notes for a summary,
    155
Using connectors 109
Using description in a
    narrative, 75
Using examples, 52
Using examples as supporting
    details, 121
Writing a concluding sentence,
    53
Writing complete sentences, 8
Writing topic sentences, 31

Mechanics

Comma splices, 132
Commas, 99
Connectors, 109
Editing symbols, 192
Indenting, 17
Margins, 17
Paragraph format, 17
Sentence fragments, 131
Run-on sentences, 132

Grammar

Adjectives, 75
Adverbs, 75
Adverbs that show time, 145
As a result of, 62
because, 62
because of, 181
Compound sentences, 18
Connectors, 109
Coordinating conjunctions, 18
in order to/so that, 170
Logical connectors that show
    cause and effect, 181
Main and dependent clauses, 62
Prepositional phrases that show
    time, 145
Pronouns, 96
Simple past, 76
Subjects and verbs, 9
Subject-verb agreement, 9
Time-order words, 72
Time clauses (*before* and *after*),
    85
Time clauses (*when, after,
    before, as soon as*), 146

Readings

An Anniversary to Remember,
    70
From a Distance, 164
A Gift of Music, 140
Good Things Come in Fours, 4
Happiness at Work, 128

A Healthy Education, 175
Music and Language, 152
Pizza around the World, 26
Rachael Ray: Celebrity Chef, 37
Ray Charles, 48
Seattle: A Great Place to Live,
    82
Sorry, You've Got Mail, 94
The Success of Starbucks, 117
Stay-at-Home Dads, 14
Using YouTube, 105
Whoopi Goldberg, 59

Reading Skills

Identifying details, 5, 15, 27, 38,
    49, 60, 71, 83, 95, 106, 119,
    129, 142, 153, 166, 177
Identifying main ideas, 5, 6, 15,
    27, 38, 49, 60, 71, 83, 95,
    106, 118, 129, 141, 153, 165,
    176
Identifying supporting
    sentences, 28
Making inferences, 142
Recognizing examples, 50
Recognizing facts and opinions,
    166
Recognizing time order in a
    narrative, 72
Skimming, 116
Understanding pronoun
    references, 96

Discussion

2, 12, 24, 35, 46, 57, 68, 80, 92,
    103, 114, 126, 138, 150, 162,
    173

Vocabulary

3, 13, 16, 25, 30, 36, 39, 47, 51,
    58, 61, 69, 74, 81, 84, 93,
    97, 104, 107, 115, 120, 127,
    130, 139, 144, 151, 154, 163,
    167, 174, 178